ArMaan Sirz Classes
Mathematics
Study Material
Class 12th

Study Material

Class XII

Subject-Mathematics

Prepared By : Muzzafar Ahmad Badder

Incoperation with : ArMaan Sirz Classes

e-mail : armaansirzclasses@gmail.com

We feel satisfied in presenting this content for you. We take an opportunity to present this content entitled as " **Mathematics Class XII Study Material by ArMaan Sirz Classes** " to the students studying in Class XII and preparing for competitive exams.

While writing this book, we have constantly kept in mind the latest examination requirements of students studying in Class XII and preparing for competitive exams. In short, it is hoped that the book will embrace the requirements of all the students and will earn appreciation of all the fellow teachers. Although every care has been taken to check the mistakes and misprints, yet it is difficult to claim perfection. Any errors, omissions and suggestions for the improvement of this content, brought to our notice, will be thankfully acknowledged and Incorporated in future.

INDEX

ITEM	PAGE NO.	
	From	To
1. Syllabus 2022-23	2	3
2. Important Trigonometric Results & Substitutions	4	5
3. Study Material : Relations and Functions	6	10
4. Study Material : Inverse Trigonometric Functions	11	13
5. Study Material : Matrices & Determinants	14	22
6 Study Material : Continuity and Differentiability	23	29
7 Study Material : Application of Derivatives	30	39
8 Study Material : Indefinite Integrals	40	48
9. Study Material : Definite Integrals	49	54
10. Study Material : Applications of the Integrals	55	56
11. Study Material : Differential Equations	57	62
12. Study Material : Vectors	63	70
13. Study Material : Three - dimensional Geometry	71	74
14. Study Material : Linear Programming	75	77
15. Study Material : Probability	78	85
16. Multiple Choice Questions	86	104

MATHEMATICS (Code No. 041)
CLASS XII (2022-23)
COURSE STRUCTURE

One Paper　　　　　　　　　　　　　　　　　　　　　　　**Max Marks: 80**

No.	Units	Marks
I	Relations and Functions	08
II	Algebra	10
III	Calculus	35
IV.	Vectors and Three - Dimensional Geometry	14
V	Linear Programming	05
VI	Probability	08
	Total	80
	Internal Assessment	20

Unit-I: Relations and Functions
1. Relations and Functions
Types of relations: reflexive, symmetric, transitive and equivalence relations. One to one and onto functions.

2. Inverse Trigonometric Functions
Definition, range, domain, principal value branch. Graphs of inverse trigonometric functions.

Unit-II: Algebra
1. Matrices
Concept, notation, order, equality, types of matrices, zero and identity matrix, transpose of a matrix, symmetric and skew symmetric matrices. Operation on matrices: Addition and multiplication and multiplication with a scalar. Simple properties of addition, multiplication and scalar multiplication. On-commutativity of multiplication of matrices and existence of non-zero matrices whose product is the zero matrix (restrict to square matrices of order 2). Invertible matrices and proof of the uniqueness of inverse, if it exists; (Here all matrices will have real entries).

2. Determinants
Determinant of a square matrix (up to 3 x 3 matrices), minors, co-factors and applications of determinants in finding the area of a triangle. Adjoint and inverse of a square matrix. Consistency, inconsistency and number of solutions of system of linear equations by examples, solving system of linear equations in two or three variables (having unique solution) using inverse of a matrix.

Unit-III: Calculus
1. Continuity and Differentiability
Continuity and differentiability, chain rule, derivative of inverse trigonometric functions, $like \sin^{-1} x$, $\cos^{-1} x$ and $\tan^{-1} x$, derivative of implicit functions. Concept of exponential and logarithmic functions. Derivatives of logarithmic and exponential functions. Logarithmic differentiation, derivative of functions expressed in parametric forms. Second order derivatives.

2. Applications of Derivatives
Applications of derivatives: rate of change of bodies, increasing/decreasing functions, maxima and minima (first derivative test motivated geometrically and second derivative test given as a provable tool). Simple problems (that illustrate basic principles and understanding of the subject as well as real-life situations).

3. Integrals Integration as inverse process of differentiation. Integration of a variety of functions by substitution, by partial fractions and by parts, only simple integrals of the type $\int \dfrac{dx}{x^2 \pm a^2}$, $\int \dfrac{dx}{\sqrt{x^2 \pm a^2}}$, $\int \dfrac{1}{\sqrt{a^2 - x^2}}\,dx$, $\int \dfrac{dx}{ax^2 + bx + c}$, $\int \dfrac{dx}{\sqrt{ax^2 + bx + c}}$, $\int \dfrac{(px + q)dx}{ax^2 + bx + c}$, $\int \dfrac{(px + q)dx}{\sqrt{ax^2 + bx + c}}$, $\int \sqrt{a^2 \pm x^2}\,dx$, $\int \sqrt{x^2 - a^2}\,dx$, $\int \sqrt{ax^2 + bx + c}\,dx$ to be evaluated. Fundamental Theorem of Calculus (without proof). Basic properties of definite integrals and evaluation of definite integrals.

4. Applications of the Integrals
Applications in finding the area under simple curves, especially lines, circles/ parabolas/ellipses (in standard form only)

5. Differential Equations
Definition, order and degree, general and particular solutions of a differential equation. Solution of differential equations by method of separation of variables, solutions of homogeneous differential equations of first order and first degree. Solutions of linear differential equation of the type:

$$\frac{dy}{dx} + py = q, \text{ where p and q are functions of x or constants.}$$

$$\frac{dx}{dy} + px = q, \text{ where p and q are functions of y or constants.}$$

Unit-IV: Vectors and Three-Dimensional Geometry
1.Vectors
Vectors and scalars, magnitude and direction of a vector. Direction cosines and direction ratios of a vector. Types of vectors (equal, unit, zero, parallel and collinear vectors), position vector of a point, negative of a vector, components of a vector, addition of vectors, multiplication of a vector by a scalar, position vector of a point dividing a line segment in a given ratio. Definition, Geometrical Interpretation, properties and application of scalar (dot) product of vectors, vector (cross) product of vectors.

2. Three - dimensional Geometry
Direction cosines and direction ratios of a line joining two points. Cartesian equation and vector equation of a line, skew lines, shortest distance between two lines. Angle between two lines.

Unit-V: Linear Programming
1.Linear Programming
Introduction, related terminology such as constraints, objective function, optimization, graphical method of solution for problems in two variables, feasible and infeasible regions (bounded or unbounded), feasible and infeasible solutions, optimal feasible solutions (up to three non-trivial constraints).

Unit-VI: Probability
1.Probability 30 Periods Conditional probability, multiplication theorem on probability, independent events, total probability, Bayes' theorem, Random variable and its probability distribution, mean of random variable

IMPORTANT TRIGONOMETRIC RESULTS & SUBSTITUTIONS

** Formulae for t-ratios of Allied Angles :

All T-ratio changes in $\frac{\pi}{2} \pm \theta$ and $\frac{3\pi}{2} \pm \theta$ while remains unchanged in $\pi \pm \theta$ and $2\pi \pm \theta$.

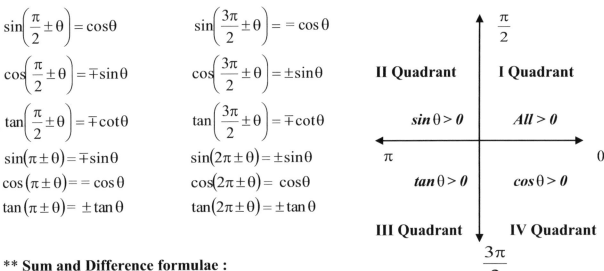

$$\sin\left(\frac{\pi}{2} \pm \theta\right) = \cos\theta \qquad \sin\left(\frac{3\pi}{2} \pm \theta\right) = = \cos\theta$$

$$\cos\left(\frac{\pi}{2} \pm \theta\right) = \mp\sin\theta \qquad \cos\left(\frac{3\pi}{2} \pm \theta\right) = \pm\sin\theta$$

$$\tan\left(\frac{\pi}{2} \pm \theta\right) = \mp\cot\theta \qquad \tan\left(\frac{3\pi}{2} \pm \theta\right) = \mp\cot\theta$$

$$\sin(\pi \pm \theta) = \mp\sin\theta \qquad \sin(2\pi \pm \theta) = \pm\sin\theta$$

$$\cos(\pi \pm \theta) = = \cos\theta \qquad \cos(2\pi \pm \theta) = \cos\theta$$

$$\tan(\pi \pm \theta) = \pm\tan\theta \qquad \tan(2\pi \pm \theta) = \pm\tan\theta$$

Quadrant diagram:

II Quadrant — I Quadrant
$\sin\theta > 0$ — $All > 0$
III Quadrant — IV Quadrant
$\tan\theta > 0$ — $\cos\theta > 0$

with $\frac{\pi}{2}$ at top, π at left, 0 at right, $\frac{3\pi}{2}$ at bottom.

** Sum and Difference formulae :

$\sin(A + B) = \sin A \cos B + \cos A \sin B$

$\sin(A - B) = \sin A \cos B - \cos A \sin B$

$\cos(A + B) = \cos A \cos B - \sin A \sin B$

$\cos(A - B) = \cos A \cos B + \sin A \sin B$

$$\tan(A + B) = \frac{\tan A + \tan B}{1 - \tan A \tan B}, \quad \tan(A - B) = \frac{\tan A - \tan B}{1 + \tan A \tan B}, \quad \tan\left(\frac{\pi}{4} + A\right) = \frac{1 + \tan A}{1 - \tan A},$$

$$\tan\left(\frac{\pi}{4} - A\right) = \frac{1 - \tan A}{1 + \tan A}, \quad \cot(A + B) = \frac{\cot A . \cot B - 1}{\cot B + \cot A} \qquad \cot(A - B) = \frac{\cot A . \cot B + 1}{\cot B - \cot A}$$

$\sin(A + B)\sin(A - B) = \sin^2 A - \sin^2 B = \cos^2 B - \cos^2 A$

$\cos(A + B)\cos(A - B) = \cos^2 A - \sin^2 B = \cos^2 B - \sin^2 A$

**Formulae for the transformation of a product of two circular functions into algebraic sum of two circular functions and vice-versa.

$2 \sin A \cos B = \sin(A + B) + \sin(A - B)$

$2 \cos A \sin B = \sin(A + B) - \sin(A - B)$

$2 \cos A \cos B = \cos(A + B) + \cos(A - B)$

$2 \sin A \sin B = \cos(A - B) - \cos(A + B)$

$$\sin C + \sin D = 2 \sin\frac{C + D}{2} \cos\frac{C - D}{2}, \qquad \sin C - \sin D = 2 \cos\frac{C + D}{2} \sin\frac{C - D}{2}.$$

$$\cos C + \cos D = 2 \cos\frac{C + D}{2} \cos\frac{C - D}{2}, \qquad \cos C - \cos D = -2 \sin\frac{C + D}{2} \sin\frac{C - D}{2}.$$

** Formulae for t-ratios of múltiple and sub-múltiple angles :

$$\sin 2A = 2 \sin A \cos A = \frac{2 \tan A}{1 + \tan^2 A}.$$

$$\cos 2A = \cos^2 A - \sin^2 A = 1 - 2 \sin^2 A = 2 \cos^2 A - 1 = \frac{1 - \tan^2 A}{1 + \tan^2 A}$$

$$1 + \cos 2A = 2\cos^2 A \qquad 1 - \cos 2A = 2\sin^2 A \qquad 1 + \cos A = 2\cos^2 \frac{A}{2} \qquad 1 - \cos A = 2\sin^2 \frac{A}{2}$$

$$\tan 2A = \frac{2\tan A}{1 - \tan^2 A}, \qquad\qquad\qquad \tan 3A = \frac{3\tan A - \tan^3 A}{1 - 3\tan^2 A}.$$

$$\sin 3A = 3\sin A - 4\sin^3 A, \qquad\qquad \cos 3A = 4\cos^3 A - 3\cos A$$

$$\sin 15° = \cos 75° = \frac{\sqrt{3} - 1}{2\sqrt{2}}. \qquad\qquad \& \qquad \cos 15° = \sin 75° = \frac{\sqrt{3} + 1}{2\sqrt{2}},$$

$$\tan 15° = \frac{\sqrt{3} - 1}{\sqrt{3} + 1} = 2 - \sqrt{3} = \cot 75° \qquad \& \qquad \tan 75° = \frac{\sqrt{3} + 1}{\sqrt{3} - 1} = 2 + \sqrt{3} = \cot 15°.$$

$$\sin 18° = \frac{\sqrt{5} - 1}{4} = \cos 72° \qquad\qquad \text{and } \cos 36° = \frac{\sqrt{5} + 1}{4} = \sin 54°.$$

$$\sin 36° = \frac{\sqrt{10 - 2\sqrt{5}}}{4} = \cos 54° \qquad\qquad \text{and } \cos 18° = \frac{\sqrt{10 + 2\sqrt{5}}}{4} = \sin 72°.$$

$$\tan\left(22\frac{1}{2}\right)° = \sqrt{2} - 1 = \cot 67\frac{1}{2}° \qquad \text{and } \tan\left(67\frac{1}{2}\right)° = \sqrt{2} + 1 = \cot\left(22\frac{1}{2}\right)°.$$

** Properties of Triangles : In any Δ ABC,

$$\frac{a}{\sin A} = \frac{b}{\sin B} = \frac{c}{\sin C} \quad \text{[Sine Formula]}$$

$$\cos A = \frac{b^2 + c^2 - a^2}{2bc}, \quad \cos B = \frac{c^2 + a^2 - b^2}{2ca}, \quad \cos C = \frac{a^2 + b^2 - c^2}{2ab}.$$

** Projection Formulae : $a = b\cos C + c\cos B, \quad b = c\cos A + a\cos C, \quad c = a\cos B + b\cos A$

** Some important trigonometric substitutions :

$\sqrt{a^2 + x^2}$	Put $x = a\tan\theta$ or $a\cot\theta$
$\sqrt{x^2 - a^2}$	Put $x = a\sec\theta$ or $a\,\mathrm{cosec}\,\theta$
$\sqrt{a + x}$ or $\sqrt{a - x}$ or both	Put $x = a\cos 2\theta$
$\sqrt{a^n + x^n}$ or $\sqrt{a^n - x^n}$ or both	Put $x^n = a^n \cos 2\theta$
$\sqrt{1 + \sin 2\theta}$	$= \sin\theta + \cos\theta$
$\sqrt{1 - \sin 2\theta}$	$= \cos\theta - \sin\theta, \ 0 < \theta < \frac{\pi}{4}$
	$= \sin\theta - \cos\theta, \ \frac{\pi}{4} < \theta < \frac{\pi}{2}$

**General solutions:

$$*\cos\theta = 0 \Rightarrow \theta = n\pi, \ n \in Z$$

$$*\sin\theta = 0 \Rightarrow \theta = (2n + 1)\frac{\pi}{2}, \ n \in Z$$

$$*\tan\theta = 0 \Rightarrow \theta = n\pi, \ n \in Z$$

$$*\sin\theta = \sin\alpha \Rightarrow \theta = n\pi + (-1)^n \alpha, \ n \in Z$$

$$*\cos\theta = \cos\alpha \Rightarrow \theta = 2n\pi \pm \alpha, \ n \in Z$$

$$*\tan\theta = \tan\alpha \Rightarrow \theta = n\pi + \alpha, \ n \in Z$$

RELATIONS AND FUNCTIONS
SOME IMPORTANT RESULTS/CONCEPTS

** **Relation :** A relation R from a non-empty set A to a non-empty set B is a subset of $A \times B$.

A **relation R in a set A is called

    (i) **Reflexive**, if $(a, a) \in R$, for every $a \in A$,

    (ii) **Symmetric**, if $(a, b) \in R$ then $(b, a) \in R$,

    (iii) **Transitive**, if $(a, b) \in R$ and $(b, c) \in R$ then $(a, c) \in R$.

** **Equivalence Relation :** R is equivalence if it is reflexive, symmetric and transitive.

** **Function :** A relation $f : A \rightarrow B$ is said to be a function if every element of A is correlated to unique element in B.

    * A is domain

    * B is codomain

* For any x element $x \in A$, function **f** correlates it to an element in B, which is denoted by f(x) and is called image of x under **f** . Again if $y = f(x)$, then x is called as pre- image of y.

* Range = $\{f(x) \mid x \in A\}$. Range $\subseteq$ Codomain

* The largest possible domain of a function is called domain of definition.

Composite function : Let two functions be defined as $f : A \rightarrow B$ and $g : B \rightarrow C$. Then we can define a function **gof**: $A \rightarrow C$ is called the composite function of **f** and **g**.

** **Different type of functions :** Let $f : A \rightarrow B$ be a function.

    ***f** is **one to one (injective) mapping**, if any two different elements in A is always correlated to different elements in B, i.e. $x_1 \neq x_2 \Rightarrow f(x_1) \neq f(x_2)$ or $f(x_1) = f(x_2) \Rightarrow x_1 = x_2$

    ***f** is **many one mapping**, if $\exists$ at least two elements in A such that their images are same.

    ***f** is **onto mapping** (subjective), if each element in B is having at least one pre image.

    ***f** is **into mapping** if range $\subseteq$ codomain.

    * f is **bijective mapping** if it is both one to one and onto.

SOME ILUSTRATIONS :

(a) Let A ={1, 2, 3}, then

  (i) R = {(1 , 1), (2 , 2), (3 , 3), (1 , 2), (2 , 3) } is reflexive but neither symmetric nor transitive.

    As (1 , 1), (2 , 2), (3 , 3) $\in R$, (1 , 2) $\in R$ but (2 , 1) $\notin R$, and (1 , 2), (2 , 3) $\in R$ but (1 , 3) $\notin R$

  (ii) R = {(1 , 1), (2 , 2), (1 , 2), (2 , 3)} is neither reflexive nor symmetric nor transitive.

    As (3 , 3) $\notin R$, (1 , 2) $\in R$ but (2 , 1) $\notin R$, and (1 , 2), (2 , 3) $\in R$ but (1 , 3) $\notin R$

 (iii) R = {(1 , 1), (2 , 2), (3 , 3), (1 , 2), (2 , 1), (2 , 3), (3 , 2), (1 , 3), (3 , 1)} is reflexive, symmetric and transitive (Equivalence Relation) as (a, a) $\in R$, for every $a \in A$, (a, b) $\in R$ then (b , a) $\in R$ and (a , b) $\in R$ and (b , c) $\in R$ then (a , c) $\in R$.

(b) The relation R in the set **Z** of integers given by R = {(a , b) : 2 divides a – b} is an equivalence relation.

Given R = {(a , b) : 2 divides a – b}

<u>Reflexive</u> $\because$ a – a = 0, divisible by 2, $\forall a \in A$

    $\therefore$ (a , a) $\in A$, $\forall a \in A$ $\Rightarrow$ R is reflexive.

<u>Symmetric :</u> Let (a , b) $\in R \Rightarrow$ 2 divides a – b , say a – b = 2m

        $\Rightarrow$ b – a = –2m

        $\Rightarrow$ 2 divides b – a

        $\Rightarrow$ (b , a) $\in R$ $\Rightarrow$ R is symmetric.

6

<u>Transitive:</u> Let $(a, b), (b, c) \in R$

$\Rightarrow$ 2 divides $a - b$, say $a - b = 2m$

$\Rightarrow$ 2 divides $b - c$, say $a - b = 2n$

$a - b + b - c = 2m + 2n$

$\Rightarrow a - c = 2(m + n)$ $\Rightarrow$ 2 divides $a - c$.

$\Rightarrow (a, c) \in R$. $\Rightarrow R$ is Transitive.

$\because$ R is reflexive, symmetric and transitive.

$\therefore$ R is an equivalence relation.

(c) Let $A = \mathbf{R} - \{3\}$ and $B = \mathbf{R} - \{1\}$. Consider the function $f : A \to B$ defined by $f(x) = \left(\dfrac{x-2}{x-3}\right)$ is one-one and onto.

Sol. $f : \mathbf{R} \to \mathbf{R}$ is given by, $f(x) = \left(\dfrac{x-2}{x-3}\right)$.

Let $f(x_1) = f(x_2) \Rightarrow \left(\dfrac{x_1-2}{x_1-3}\right) = \left(\dfrac{x_2-2}{x_2-3}\right)$

$\Rightarrow x_1 x_2 - 3x_1 - 2x_2 + 6 = x_1 x_2 - 3x_2 - 2x_1 + 6$

$\Rightarrow x_1 = x_2$ $\Rightarrow$ f is a one-one

Let $y = f(x) = \dfrac{x-2}{x-3} \Rightarrow xy - 3y = x - 2 \Rightarrow x = \dfrac{3y-2}{y-1}$

Therefore, for any $y \in B$, there exists $\dfrac{3y-2}{y-1} \in A$

$\Rightarrow$ f is onto.

$\therefore$ f is one-one and onto.

SHORT ANSWER TYPE QUESTIONS

1. Let $A = \{1, 2, 3\}$ and consider the relation $R = \{1, 1), (2, 2), (3, 3), (1, 2), (2, 3), (2,1)\}$. Then determine whether R is reflexive, symmetric and transitive.

2. Let $A = \{1, 2, 3\}$ and consider the relation $R = \{1, 1), (2, 2), (3, 3), (1, 2), (2, 3), (1,3), (3, 1)\}$. Then determine whether R is reflexive, symmetric and transitive.

3. Let $A = \{1, 2, 3\}$ and consider the relation $R = \{1, 1), (2, 2), (3, 3), (1, 2), (2, 1)\}$. Then determine whether R is reflexive, symmetric and transitive.

4. Let $A = \{1, 2, 3\}$ and consider the relation $R = \{(1, 1), (1, 2), (2, 1)\}$. Then determine whether R is reflexive, symmetric and transitive.

5. Let $A = \{1, 2, 3\}$ and consider the relation $R = \{(1, 3)\}$. Then determine whether R is reflexive, symmetric and transitive.

6. Let $A = \{1, 2, 3\}$ and consider the relation $R = \{1, 1), (2, 2), (3, 3)\}$. Then determine whether R is reflexive, symmetric and transitive.

7. Let $A = \{1, 2, 3\}$ and $R = \{(1, 1), (2, 3), (1, 2)\}$ be a relation on A, then write the minimum number of ordered pairs to be added in **R** to make **R** reflexive and transitive.

8. Write the maximum number of equivalence relations on the set $\{1, 2, 3\}$.

9. Let R be a relation on the set N be defined by $\{(x, y) : x, y \in N, 2x + y = 41\}$. Then determine whether R is reflexive, symmetric and transitive.

10. Relation R in the set **Z** of all integers defined as R = {(x, y) : x – y is an even integer}. Determine whether R is reflexive, symmetric and transitive.

11. Let R be the relation on the set of all real numbers defined by a R b iff |a – b| ≤ 1. Then determine whether R is reflexive, symmetric and transitive.

12. . Relation R in the set A = {1, 2, 3, 4, 5, 6, 7, 8} as R = {(x, y) : x divides y}. Determine whether R is reflexive, symmetric and transitive.

13. Let L denote the set of all straight lines in a plane. Let a relation R be defined by l_1 R l_2 if and only if l_1 is perpendicular to l_2 ,∀ l_1, l_2 ∈ L. Determine whether R is reflexive, symmetric and transitive.

14. If A = {a, b, c} then find the number of relations containing (a , b) and (a , c) which are reflexive and symmetric but not transitive.

15. The relation R in the set {1, 2, 3, ... , 13, 14} is defined by R = {(x , y) : 3x – y = 0}. Determine whether R is reflexive, symmetric and transitive.

16. The relation R in the set of natural numbers N is defined by R = {(x , y) : x > y}. Determine whether R is reflexive, symmetric and transitive.

17. Write the condition for which the function f : X → Y is one-one (or injective).

18. Write the condition for which the function f : X → Y is said to be onto (or surjective).

19. When a function f : X → Y is said to be bijective ?

20. If a set A contains **m** elements and the set B contains **n** elements with n > m, then write the number of bijective functions from A to B.

21. Let X = {– 1, 0, 1}, Y = {0, 2} and a function f : X →Y defined by $y = 2x^4$. Is f one-one and onto?

22. Let $f(x) = x^2 – 4x – 5$. Is f one-one on R ?

23. The function f : R → R given by $f(x) = x^2$, x ∈R where R is the set of real numbers. Is f one-one and onto?

24. The signum function, f : R → R is given by $f(x) = \begin{cases} 1 ,\text{if } x > 0 \\ 0, \text{if } x = 0 \\ -1, \text{if } x < 0 \end{cases}$. Is f one-one and onto?

25. Let f : R → R be defined by $f(x) = \begin{cases} 3x , & \text{if } x \leq 1 \\ x^2, & \text{if } 1 < x \leq 3 \\ 2x, & \text{if } x > 3 \end{cases}$, then find f (– 1) + f (2) + f (4).

26. Is the greatest integer function f : R → R be defined by f(x) = [x] one-one and onto?

27. Is the function f : N → N, where N is the set of natural numbers is defined by

$f(x) = \begin{cases} n^2, & \text{if } n \text{ is odd} \\ n^2 +1, & \text{if } n \text{ is even} \end{cases}$ one-one and onto?

28. Find the total number of injective mappings from a set with m elements to a set with n elements, m ≤ n.

ANSWERS

1. Reflexive but neither symmetric nor transitive   **2.** Reflexive and transitive but not symmetric

3. Reflexive, symmetric and transitive   **4.** Symmetric but neither reflexive nor transitive

5. Transitive only   **6.** Reflexive and symmetric and transitive

7. 3   **8.** 5

9. Neither reflexive nor symmetric nor transitive   **10.** Reflexive and symmetric and transitive

11. Reflexive and symmetric but not transitive   **12.** Reflexive and transitive but not symmetric

13. Symmetric only.   **14.** 1

15. Neither reflexive nor symmetric nor transitive   **16.** Transitive but neither reflexive nor symmetric

17. $\forall \ x_1, x_2 \in X, \ f(x_1) = f(x_2) \Rightarrow x_1 = x_2, \ \textbf{OR} \ x_1 \neq x_2 \Rightarrow f(x_1) \neq f(x_2)$.

18. if $\forall \ y \in Y, \ \exists$ some $x \in X$ such that $y = f(x)$ **OR** range of $f = Y$

19. If f **is** one-one and onto   **20.** 0

21. onto but not one-one(many-one onto)   **22.** f is not one-one on R

23. neither one-one nor onto   **24.** neither one-one nor onto

25. 9   **26.** neither one-one nor onto

27. one-one but not onto   **28.** $\dfrac{n!}{(n-m)!}$

LONG ANSWER TYPE QUESTIONS

RELATIONS

1. Let L be the set of all lines in a plane and R be the relation in L defined as
$R = \{(L_1, L_2) : L_1$ is perpendicular to $L_2\}$. Show that R is symmetric but neither reflexive nor transitive.

2. Show that the relation R in the set $\mathbf{Z}$ of integers given by $R = \{(a, b) : 2$ divides $a - b\}$ is an equivalence relation.

3. Let R be the relation defined in the set $A = \{1, 2, 3, 4, 5, 6, 7\}$ by $R = \{(a, b) :$ both a and b are either odd or even$\}$. Show that R is an equivalence relation. Further, show that all the elements of the subset $\{1, 3, 5, 7\}$ are related to each other and all the elements of the subset $\{2, 4, 6\}$ are related to each other, but no element of the subset $\{1, 3, 5, 7\}$ is related to any element of the subset $\{2, 4, 6\}$.

4. Show that the relation R in the set $\mathbf{R}$ of real numbers, defined as $R = \{(a, b) : a \leq b^2\}$ is neither reflexive nor symmetric nor transitive.

5. Check whether the relation R defined in the set $\{1, 2, 3, 4, 5, 6\}$ as $R = \{(a, b) : b = a + 1\}$ is reflexive, symmetric or transitive.

6. Show that the relation R in $\mathbf{R}$ defined as $R = \{(a, b) : a \leq b\}$, is reflexive and transitive but not symmetric.

7. Check whether the relation R in $\mathbf{R}$ defined by $R = \{(a, b) : a \leq b^3\}$ is reflexive, symmetric or transitive.

8. Show that the relation R in the set $A = \{1, 2, 3, 4, 5\}$ given by $R = \{(a, b) : |a - b|$ is even$\}$, is an equivalence relation. Show that all the elements of $\{1, 3, 5\}$ are related to each other and all the elements of $\{2, 4\}$ are

related to each other. But no element of $\{1, 3, 5\}$ is related to any element of $\{2, 4\}$.

9. Show that each of the relation R in the set

 $A = \{x \in \mathbf{Z} : 0 \leq x \leq 12\}$, given by $R = \{(a, b) : |a - b|$ is a multiple of 4$\}$ is an equivalence relation. Find the set of all elements related to 1.

10. Show that the relation R in the set A of points in a plane given by $R = \{(P, Q) :$ distance of the point P from the origin is same as the distance of the point Q from the origin$\}$, is an equivalence relation. Further, show that the set of all points related to a point $P \neq (0, 0)$ is the circle passing through P with origin as centre.

11. Show that the relation R defined in the set A of all triangles as $R = \{(T_1, T_2) : T_1$ is similar to $T_2\}$, is equivalence relation. Consider three right angle triangles T1 with sides 3, 4, 5, T_2 with sides 5, 12, 13 and T_3 with sides 6, 8, 10. Which triangles among T_1, T_2 and T_3 are related?

12. Show that the relation R defined in the set A of all polygons as $R = \{(P_1, P_2) : P_1$ and P_2 have same number of sides$\}$, is an equivalence relation. What is the set of all elements in A related to the right angle triangle T with sides 3, 4 and 5?

13. Let L be the set of all lines in XY plane and R be the relation in L defined as

9

R = {(L₁, L₂) : L₁ is parallel to L₂}. Show that R is an equivalence relation. Find the set of all lines related to the line $y = 2x + 4$.

14. If R_1 and R_2 are equivalence relations in a set A, show that $R_1 \cap R_2$ is also an equivalence relation.

15. Let R be a relation on the set A of ordered pairs of positive integers defined by $(x, y) R (u, v)$ if and only if $xv = yu$. Show that R is an equivalence relation.

16. Let $f : X \rightarrow Y$ be a function. Define a relation R in X given by $R = \{(a, b): f(a) = f(b)\}$. Examine if R is an equivalence relation.

17. Given a non empty set X, consider P(X) which is the set of all subsets of X. Define the relation R in P(X) as follows: For subsets A, B in P(X), ARB if and only if $A \subset B$. Is R an equivalence relation on P(X)? Justify your answer.

FUNCTIONS

1. Prove that the Greatest Integer Function $f : \mathbf{R} \rightarrow \mathbf{R}$, given by $f(x) = [x]$, is neither one-one nor onto, where $[x]$ denotes the greatest integer less than or equal to x.

2. Show that the Modulus Function $f : \mathbf{R} \rightarrow \mathbf{R}$, given by $f(x) = |x|$, is neither one-one nor onto, where $|x|$ is x, if x is positive or 0 and $|x|$ is $-x$, if x is negative.

3. In each of the following cases, state whether the function is one-one, onto or bijective. Justify your answer. (i) $f : \mathbf{R} \rightarrow \mathbf{R}$ defined by $f(x) = 3 - 4x$ (ii) $f : \mathbf{R} \rightarrow \mathbf{R}$ defined by $f(x) = 1 + x^2$.

4. Let A and B be sets. Show that $f : A \times B \rightarrow B \times A$ such that $f(a, b) = (b, a)$ is bijective function.

5. Let $f : \mathbf{N} \rightarrow \mathbf{N}$ be defined by

$$f(n) = \begin{cases} \dfrac{n+1}{2}, & \text{if n is odd} \\ \dfrac{n}{2}, & \text{if n is even} \end{cases} \quad \text{for all } n \in N$$

State whether the function f is bijective. Justify your answer.

6. Let $A = \mathbf{R} - \{3\}$ and $B = \mathbf{R} - \{1\}$. Consider the function $f : A \rightarrow B$ defined by $f(x) = \left(\dfrac{x-2}{x-3}\right)$.

Is f one-one and onto? Justify your answer.

7. Consider $f : \mathbf{R} \rightarrow \mathbf{R}$ given by $f(x) = 4x + 3$. Show that f is one-one and onto.

8. Consider $f : \mathbf{R+} \rightarrow [-5, \infty)$ given by $f(x) = 9x^2 + 6x - 5$. Show that f is one-one and onto..

9. Show that $f : \mathbf{N} \rightarrow \mathbf{N}$, given by $f(x) = \begin{cases} x+1, & \text{if x is odd} \\ x-1, & \text{if x is even} \end{cases}$ is both one-one and onto.

INVERSE TRIGONOMETRIC FUNCTIONS

* Domain & Range of the Inverse Trigonometric Function :

Functions	Domain	Range (Principal value Branch)
$\sin^{-1}$	$[-1,1]$	$[-\pi/2, \pi/2]$
$\cos^{-1}$:	$[-1,1]$	$[0, \pi]$
cosec^{-1} :	$R-(-1, 1)$	$[-\pi/2, \pi/2]-\{0\}$
$\sec^{-1}$:	$R-(-1, 1)$	$[0, \pi]-\{\pi/2\}$
$\tan^{-1}$:	R	$(-\pi/2, \pi/2)$
$\cot^{-1}$:	R	$(0, \pi)$

* Properties of Inverse Trigonometric Function

1. i $\sin^{-1}(\sin x)=x$, $x \in [-\pi/2, \pi/2]$ & $\sin(\sin^{-1}x)=x$, $x \in [-1,1]$

   ii. $\cos^{-1}(\cos x)=x$, $x \in [0, \pi]$ & $\cos(\cos^{-1}x)=x$, $x \in [-1,1]$

   iii. $\tan^{-1}(\tan x)=x$, $x \in (-\pi/2, \pi/2)$ & $\tan(\tan^{-1}x)=x$, $x \in R$

   iv. $\cot^{-1}(\cot x)=x$, $x \in (0, \pi)$ & $\cot(\cot^{-1}x)=x$, $x \in R$

   v. $\sec^{-1}(\sec x)=x$, $x \in [0, \pi]-\pi/2$ & $\sec(\sec^{-1}x)=x$ $x \in R-(-1, 1)$

   vi. $\text{cosec}^{-1}(\text{cosec}\,x)=x$, $[-\pi/2, \pi/2]-\{0\}$ & $\text{cosec}(\text{cosec}^{-1}x)=x \in R-[-1, 1]$

2. i. $\sin^{-1}x = \text{cosec}^{-1}\dfrac{1}{x}$ & $\sin^{-1}x = \text{cosec}^{-1}\dfrac{1}{x}$

   ii. $\cos^{-1}x = \sec^{-1}\dfrac{1}{x}$ & $\sec^{-1}x = \cos^{-1}\dfrac{1}{x}$

   iii. $\tan^{-1}x = \cot^{-1}\dfrac{1}{x}$ & $\cot^{-1}x = \tan^{-1}\dfrac{1}{x}$

3. i $\sin^{-1}(-x)=-\sin^{-1}x$ ii. $\tan^{-1}(-x)=-\tan^{-1}x$ iii. $\text{cosec}^{-1}(-x)=-\text{cosec}^{-1}x$

   iv $\cos^{-1}(-x)=\pi-\cos^{-1}x$ v $\sec^{-1}(-x)=\pi-\sec^{-1}x$ vi $\cot^{-1}(-x)=\pi-\cot^{-1}x$

SOME ILUSTRATIONS :

1. Domain of $\cos^{-1}(2x-1)$ is $[0, 1]$

   As $-1 \le 2x-1 \le 1 \Rightarrow 0 \le 2x \le 2 \Rightarrow 0 \le x \le 1$

2. Principal value of $\cos^{-1}\left(-\dfrac{\sqrt{3}}{2}\right)$ is equal to $\dfrac{5\pi}{6}$

   As $\cos^{-1}\left(-\dfrac{\sqrt{3}}{2}\right) = \pi - \cos^{-1}\left(\dfrac{\sqrt{3}}{2}\right) = \pi - \dfrac{\pi}{6} = \dfrac{5\pi}{6}$

3. Principal value of $\sin^{-1}\left(\dfrac{\sqrt{3}-1}{2\sqrt{2}}\right)$ is equal to $\dfrac{\pi}{12}$

11

As $\sin^{-1}\left(\dfrac{\sqrt{3}-1}{2\sqrt{2}}\right) = \sin^{-1}\left(\dfrac{\sqrt{3}}{2}\cdot\dfrac{1}{\sqrt{2}} - \dfrac{1}{2}\cdot\dfrac{1}{\sqrt{2}}\right) = \sin^{-1}\left(\sin\dfrac{\pi}{3}\cdot\cos\dfrac{\pi}{4} - \cos\dfrac{\pi}{3}\cdot\sin\dfrac{\pi}{4}\right) = \sin^{-1}\left(\sin\dfrac{\pi}{12}\right) = \dfrac{\pi}{12}$

SHORT ANSWER TYPE QUESTIONS

1. Find the domain of $\sin^{-1}(2x-1)$.

2. Find the domain of $\sin^{-1}x + \cos x$.

3. Find the domain of $\sin^{-1}\sqrt{x-1}$.

4. Find the principal value of $\sec^{-1}(-2)$.

5. Find the principal value of $\sin^{-1}\left(\cos\dfrac{2\pi}{3}\right)$.

6. Find the principal value of $\tan^{-1}\left(\tan\dfrac{15\pi}{4}\right)$.

7. Find the principal value of $\sec^{-1}\left(2\sin\dfrac{3\pi}{4}\right)$.

8. Find the principal value of $\cot^{-1}\left(\tan\dfrac{3\pi}{4}\right)$.

9. Find the principal value of $\cos^{-1}\left(\cos\dfrac{3\pi}{2}\right)$.

10. Find the principal value of $\sin^{-1}\left(\cos\dfrac{33\pi}{5}\right)$.

11. Find the principal value of $\sin^{-1}\left(\sin\dfrac{3\pi}{5}\right)$.

12. Find the principal value of $\cos^{-1}\left(\dfrac{\sqrt{3}+1}{2\sqrt{2}}\right)$.

13. Find the value of $\cos(\sin^{-1}x)$.

14. Find the value of $\cot(\cos^{-1}x)$.

15. Find the value of $\sin^{-1}\left\{\cos(\sin^{-1}\dfrac{\sqrt{3}}{2})\right\}$.

16. Find the value of $\tan^{-1}\left\{2\cos\left(2\sin^{-1}\dfrac{1}{2}\right)\right\}$.

17. Find the value of $\cot\left[\sin^{-1}\left\{\cos\left(\tan^{-1}1\right)\right\}\right]$.

18. Find the value of $\tan^{-1}\left\{2\sin\left(4\cos^{-1}\dfrac{\sqrt{3}}{2}\right)\right\}$.

19. Find the value of $\cos^{-1}\left(\cos\dfrac{2\pi}{3}\right) + \sin^{-1}\left(\sin\dfrac{2\pi}{3}\right)$.

20. Find the value of $\tan^{-1}\left(\tan\dfrac{5\pi}{6}\right) + \cos^{-1}\left(\cos\dfrac{13\pi}{6}\right)$.

ANSWERS

1. $[1, 2]$ **2.** $[-1, 1]$ **3.** $[1, 2]$ **4.** $\dfrac{2\pi}{3}$ **5.** $-\dfrac{\pi}{6}$

6. $-\dfrac{\pi}{4}$ **7.** $\dfrac{\pi}{4}$ **8.** $\dfrac{3\pi}{4}$ **9.** $\dfrac{\pi}{2}$ **10.** $-\dfrac{\pi}{10}$

11. $\dfrac{2\pi}{5}$ **12.** $\dfrac{\pi}{12}$ **13.** $\sqrt{1-x^2}$ **14.** $\dfrac{x}{\sqrt{1-x^2}}$ **15.** $\dfrac{\pi}{6}$

16. $\dfrac{\pi}{4}$ **17.** 1 **18.** $\dfrac{\pi}{3}$ **19.** π **20.** 0

MATRICES & DETERMINANTS

A matrix is a rectangular array of $m \times n$ numbers arranged in m rows and n columns.

$$A = \begin{bmatrix} a_{11} & a_{12}\ldots\ldots\ldots a_{1n} \\ a_{21} & a_{22}\ldots\ldots\ldots a_{2n} \\ & \\ a_{m1} & a_{m2}\ldots\ldots\ldots a_{mn} \end{bmatrix}_{m \times n}$$ $\rightarrow$ **ROWS**

$\downarrow$**COLUMNS**

OR

$A = [a_{ij}]_{m \times n}$, where **i** = 1, 2,...., m ; **j** = 1, 2,....,n.

* **Row Matrix**: A matrix which has one row is called row matrix. $A = [a_{ij}]_{1 \times n}$

* **Column Matrix** : A matrix which has one column is called column matrix. $A = [a_{ij}]_{m \times 1}$.

* **Square Matrix**: A matrix in which number of rows are equal to number of columns, is called a square matrix $A = [a_{ij}]_{m \times m}$

* **Diagonal Matrix** : A square matrix is called a Diagonal Matrix if all the elements, except the diagonal elements are zero. $A = [a_{ij}]_{n \times n}$, where $a_{ij} = 0$,$i \neq j$. $a_{ij} \neq 0$,$i = j$.

* **Scalar Matrix**: A square matrix is called scalar matrix it all the elements, except diagonal elements are zero and diagonal elements are some non-zero quantity. $A = [a_{ij}]_{n \times n}$, where $a_{ij} = 0$ if $i \neq j$. and $a_{ij} = k$, $i = j$.

* **Identity or Unit Matrix** : A square matrix in which all the non diagonal elements are zero and diagonal elements are unity is called identity or unit matrix.

* **Null Matrices** : A matrices in which all element are zero.

* **Equal Matrices** : Two matrices are said to be equal if they have same order and all their corresponding elements are equal.

* **Sum of two Matrices :** If $A = [a_{ij}]$ and $B = [b_{ij}]$ are two matrices of the same order, say m × n, then, the sum of the two matrices A and B is defined as a matrix $C = [c_{ij}]_{m \times n}$, where $c_{ij} = a_{ij} + b_{ij}$, for all possible values of i and j.

* **Multiplication of a matrix :**
  $kA = k [a_{ij}]_{m \times n} = [k (a_{ij})]_{m \times n}$

* **Negative of a matrix** is denoted by –A. We define –A = (– 1) A.

* **Difference of matrices :** If $A = [a_{ij}]$, $B = [b_{ij}]$ are two matrices of the same order, say m × n, then difference A – B is defined as a matrix $D = [d_{ij}]$, where $d_{ij} = a_{ij} - b_{ij}$, for all value of i and j.

* **Properties of matrix addition :**

(i) **Commutative Law :** If A = and B are matrices of the same order, then A + B = B + A.

(ii) **Associative Law :** For any three matrices A, B &C of the same order, (A + B) + C = A + (B + C).

(iii) **Existence of identity:** Let A be an m × n matrix and O be an m × n zero matrix, then A + O = O + A = A. i.e. O is the additive identity for matrix addition.

(iv) **Existence of inverse :** Let A be any matrix, then we have another matrix as – A such that A + (– A) = (– A) + A = O. So – A is the additive inverse of A or negative of A.

* **Properties of scalar multiplication of a matrix :** If A and B be two matrices of the same order, and k and l are scalars, then

(i) k(A +B) = k A + kB,   (ii) (k + l)A = k A + l A   (iii) (k+ l) A = k A + l A

14

*Product of matrices: If A& B are two matrices, then product AB is defined, if number of column of A = number of rows of B.

i.e. $A = [a_{ij}]_{m \times n}$, $B = [b_{jk}]_{n \times p}$ then $AB = [C_{ik}]_{m \times p}$, where $C_{ik} = \sum_{j=1}^{n} a_{ij}.b_{jk}$

*Properties of multiplication of matrices :
(i) Product of matrices is not commutative. i.e. $AB \neq BA$.
(ii) Product of matrices is associative. i.e $A(BC) = (AB)C$
(iii) Product of matrices is distributive over addition i.e. $(A+B) C = AC + BC$
(iv) For every square matrix A, there exist an identity matrix of same order such that $IA = AI = A$.

* Transpose of matrix : If A is the given matrix, then the matrix obtained by interchanging the rows and columns is called the transpose of a matrix.

* Properties of Transpose :
If A & B are matrices such that their sum & product are defined, then
(i). $(A^T)^T = A$ (ii). $(A + B)^T = A^T + B^T$ (iii). $(KA^T) = K.A^T$ where K is a scalar.
(iv). $(AB)^T = B^T A^T$ (v). $(ABC)^T = C^T B^T A^T$.

* Symmetric Matrix : A square matrix is said to be symmetric if $A = A^T$ i.e. If $A = [a_{ij}]_{m \times m}$, then

$a_{ij} = a_{ji}$ for all i, j. Also elements of the symmetric matrix are symmetric about the main diagonal

* Skew symmetric Matrix : A square matrix is said to be skew symmetric if $A^T = -A$.
If $A = [a_{ij}]_{m \times m}$, then $a_{ij} = -a_{ji}$ for all i, j.

* Elementary Operation (Transformation) of a Matrix:
(i) Interchange of any two rows or two columns : $R_i \leftrightarrow R_j$, $C_i \leftrightarrow C_j$.
* Multiplication of the elements of any row or column by a non zero number:
   $R_i \rightarrow k R_i$, $C_i \rightarrow kC_i$, $k \neq 0$
* Determinant : To every square matrix we can assign a number called determinant
   If $A = [a_{11}]$,   det. $A = |A| = a_{11}$.
   If $A = \begin{bmatrix} a_{11} & a_{12} \\ a_{21} & a_{22} \end{bmatrix}$, $|A| = a_{11}a_{22} - a_{21}a_{12}$.

* Properties :
(i) The determinant of the square matrix A is unchanged when its rows and columns are interchanged.
(ii) The determinant of a square matrix obtained by interchanging two rows(or two columns) is negative of given determinant.
(iii) If two rows or two columns of a determinant are identical, value of the determinant is zero.
(iv) If allthe elements of a row or column of a square matrix A are multiplied by a non-zero number k, then determinant of the new matrix is k times the determinant of A.
(v) If elements of any one column(or row) are expressed as sum of two elements each, then determinant can be written as sum of two determinants.
(vi) Any two or more rows(or column) can be added or subtracted proportionally.
(vii) If A & B are square matrices of same order, then $|AB| = |A| |B|$
*Singular matrix: A square matrix 'A' of order 'n' is said to be singular, if $|A| = 0$.
* Non -Singular matrix : A square matrix 'A' of order 'n' is said to be non-singular, if $|A| \neq 0$.
* If A and B are nonsingular matrices of the same order, then AB and BA are also nonsingular matrices of the same order.

* Let A be a square matrix of order n × n, then $|kA| = k^n|A|$.

* **Area of a Triangle:** area of a triangle with vertices $(x_1, y_1), (x_2, y_2)$ and (x_3, y_3) = $\dfrac{1}{2}\begin{vmatrix} x_1 & y_1 & 1 \\ x_2 & y_2 & 1 \\ x_3 & y_3 & 1 \end{vmatrix}$

* Equation of a line passing through $(x_1, y_1) \& (x_2, y_2)$ is $\begin{vmatrix} x & y & 1 \\ x_1 & y_1 & 1 \\ x_2 & y_2 & 1 \end{vmatrix} = 0$

***Minor** of an element a_{ij} of a determinant is the determinant obtained by deleting its ith row and j^{th} column in which element a_{ij} lies. Minor of an element a_{ij} is denoted by M_{ij}.

* Minor of an element of a determinant of order $n(n \geq 2)$ is a determinant of order $n - 1$.

* **Cofactor** of an element a_{ij}, denoted by A_{ij} is defined by $A_{ij} = (-1)^{i+j}M_{ij}$, where M_{ij} is minor of a_{ij}.

* If elements of a row (or column) are multiplied with cofactors of any other row (or column), then their sum is zero.

***Adjoint of matrix** :

If $A = [a_{ij}]$ be a square matrix then transpose of a matrix $[A_{ij}]$, where A_{ij} is the cofactor of A_{ij} element of matrix A, is called the adjoint of A.

Adjoint of A = Adj. A = $[A_{ij}]^T$.

A(Adj.A) = (Adj. A)A = $|A|$ I.

* If A be any given square matrix of order n, then A(adjA) = (adjA) A = $|A|$ I,

* If A is a square matrix of order n, then $|adj(A)| = |A|^{n-1}$.

***Inverse of a matrix** :Inverse of a square matrix A exists, if A is non-singular or square matrix A is

said to be invertible and $A^{-1} = \dfrac{1}{|A|}$ Adj.A

***System of Linear Equations** :

$a_1x + b_1y + c_1z = d_1, \quad a_2x + b_2y + c_2z = d_2, \quad a_3x + b_3y + c_3z = d_3.$

$\begin{bmatrix} a_1 & b_2 & c_1 \\ a_2 & b_2 & c_2 \\ a_3 & b_3 & c_3 \end{bmatrix}\begin{bmatrix} x \\ y \\ z \end{bmatrix} = \begin{bmatrix} d_1 \\ d_2 \\ d_3 \end{bmatrix} \Rightarrow AX = B \Rightarrow X = A^{-1}B \; ; \; \{|A| \neq 0\}.$

***Criteria of Consistency**.

(i) If $|A| \neq 0$, then the system of equations is said to be consistent & has a unique solution.

(ii) If $|A| = 0$ and (adj. A)B = 0, then the system of equations is consistent and has infinitely many solutions.

(iii) If $|A| = 0$ and (adj. A)B $\neq$ 0, then the system of equations is inconsistent and has no solution.

SOME ILUSTRATIONS :

Q. Express $\begin{bmatrix} 3 & -2 & -4 \\ 3 & -2 & -5 \\ -1 & 1 & 2 \end{bmatrix}$ as the sum of a symmetric and skew symmetric matrix.

Sol. Let $A = \begin{bmatrix} 3 & -2 & -4 \\ 3 & -2 & -5 \\ -1 & 1 & 2 \end{bmatrix} \Rightarrow A' = \begin{bmatrix} 3 & 3 & -1 \\ -2 & -2 & 1 \\ -4 & -5 & 2 \end{bmatrix}$

Let $A = \dfrac{1}{2}(A + A') + \dfrac{1}{2}(A - A') = P + Q$

$P = \dfrac{1}{2}(A + A') = \dfrac{1}{2}\begin{bmatrix} 6 & 1 & -5 \\ 1 & -4 & -4 \\ -5 & -4 & 4 \end{bmatrix} = \begin{bmatrix} 3 & 1/2 & -5/2 \\ 1/2 & -2 & -2 \\ -5/2 & -2 & 2 \end{bmatrix}$

$P' = \begin{bmatrix} 3 & 1/2 & -5/2 \\ 1/2 & -2 & -2 \\ -5/2 & -2 & 2 \end{bmatrix} = P \Rightarrow P$ is a symmetric matrix.

$Q = \dfrac{1}{2}(A - A') = \dfrac{1}{2}\begin{bmatrix} 0 & -5 & -3 \\ 5 & 0 & -6 \\ 3 & 6 & 0 \end{bmatrix} = \begin{bmatrix} 0 & -5/2 & -3/2 \\ 5/2 & 0 & -3 \\ 3/2 & 2 & 0 \end{bmatrix}$

$Q' = \begin{bmatrix} 0 & 5/2 & 3/2 \\ -5/2 & 0 & 3 \\ -3/2 & -3 & 0 \end{bmatrix} = -Q \Rightarrow Q$ is a skew symmetric matrix.

$P + Q = \begin{bmatrix} 3 & 1/2 & -5/2 \\ 1/2 & -2 & -2 \\ -5/2 & -2 & 2 \end{bmatrix} + \begin{bmatrix} 0 & -5/2 & -3/2 \\ 5/2 & 0 & -3 \\ 3/2 & 2 & 0 \end{bmatrix} = \begin{bmatrix} 3 & -2 & -4 \\ 3 & -2 & -5 \\ -1 & 1 & 2 \end{bmatrix} = A$

Q. Show that $A = \begin{bmatrix} 2 & -3 \\ 3 & 4 \end{bmatrix}$ satisfies the equation $x^2 - 6x + 17 = 0$. Thus find A^{-1}.

Sol. $A = \begin{bmatrix} 2 & -3 \\ 3 & 4 \end{bmatrix} \Rightarrow A^2 = \begin{bmatrix} 2 & -3 \\ 3 & 4 \end{bmatrix}\begin{bmatrix} 2 & -3 \\ 3 & 4 \end{bmatrix} = \begin{bmatrix} -5 & -18 \\ 18 & 7 \end{bmatrix}$

$A^2 - 6A + 17I = \begin{bmatrix} -5 & -18 \\ 18 & 7 \end{bmatrix} - \begin{bmatrix} 12 & -18 \\ 18 & 24 \end{bmatrix} + \begin{bmatrix} 17 & 0 \\ 0 & 17 \end{bmatrix} = \begin{bmatrix} 0 & 0 \\ 0 & 0 \end{bmatrix} = 0$

$\Rightarrow A$ satisfies the equation $x^2 - 6x + 17 = 0$

$A^2 - 6A + 17I = 0 \Rightarrow 17I = -A^2 + 6A$

$\Rightarrow 17IA^{-1} = -AA.A^{-1} + 6AA^{-1} = -AI + 6I$

$\Rightarrow 17A^{-1} = -A + 6I = \begin{bmatrix} -2 & 3 \\ -3 & -4 \end{bmatrix} + \begin{bmatrix} 6 & 0 \\ 0 & 6 \end{bmatrix} = \begin{bmatrix} 4 & 3 \\ -3 & 2 \end{bmatrix}$

$\Rightarrow A^{-1} = \dfrac{1}{17}\begin{bmatrix} 4 & 3 \\ -3 & 2 \end{bmatrix}$

Q. Use the product $\begin{bmatrix} 2 & -1 & 1 \\ -1 & 2 & -1 \\ 1 & -1 & 2 \end{bmatrix}\begin{bmatrix} 3 & 1 & -1 \\ 1 & 3 & 1 \\ -1 & 1 & 3 \end{bmatrix}$ to solve

$2x - y + z = -1, \quad -x + 2y - z = 4, \quad x - y + 2z = -3.$

Sol. Let $A = \begin{bmatrix} 2 & -1 & 1 \\ -1 & 2 & -1 \\ 1 & -1 & 2 \end{bmatrix}$, $B = \begin{bmatrix} 3 & 1 & -1 \\ 1 & 3 & 1 \\ -1 & 1 & 3 \end{bmatrix}$

$AB = \begin{bmatrix} 4 & 0 & 0 \\ 0 & 4 & 0 \\ 0 & 0 & 4 \end{bmatrix} = 4I_3 \Rightarrow A\left(\frac{1}{4}B\right) = I_3 \quad \therefore A^{-1} = \frac{1}{4}B$

Given system of equations may be written as

$AX = C$, where $A = \begin{bmatrix} 2 & -1 & 1 \\ -1 & 2 & -1 \\ 1 & -1 & 2 \end{bmatrix}$, $X = \begin{bmatrix} x \\ y \\ z \end{bmatrix}$, $C = \begin{bmatrix} -1 \\ 4 \\ -3 \end{bmatrix}$

Solution is $X = A^{-1}C = \frac{1}{4}B.C$

$= \frac{1}{4}\begin{bmatrix} 3 & 1 & -1 \\ 1 & 3 & 1 \\ -1 & 1 & 3 \end{bmatrix}\begin{bmatrix} -1 \\ 4 \\ -3 \end{bmatrix} = \frac{1}{4}\begin{bmatrix} 4 \\ 8 \\ -4 \end{bmatrix} = \begin{bmatrix} 1 \\ 2 \\ -1 \end{bmatrix}$

$\therefore x = 1, y = 2, z = -1$

MATRICES
SHORT ANSWER TYPE QUESTIONS

1. Write the number of all possible matrices of order 2×2 with entries -1 or 0 or 1 ?

2. If a matrix has 12 elements, then write the number of possible orders it can have.

3. A matrix $A = \begin{bmatrix} a_{ij} \end{bmatrix}_{3\times 4}$, whose elements are given by $a_{ij} = \frac{1}{2}|i - 3j|^2$, then find the value of a_{32}.

4. If $\begin{bmatrix} 3x+7 & 5 \\ y+1 & 2-3x \end{bmatrix} = \begin{bmatrix} 2 & y-2 \\ 8 & 7 \end{bmatrix}$, then what are the values of x and y.

5. If $\begin{bmatrix} x+y & 2 \\ 5+z & xy \end{bmatrix} = \begin{bmatrix} 6 & 2 \\ 5 & 8 \end{bmatrix}$ then find the values of x, y and z .

6. If $\begin{bmatrix} 1 & 2 \\ -2 & -b \end{bmatrix} + \begin{bmatrix} a & 4 \\ 3 & 2 \end{bmatrix} = \begin{bmatrix} 5 & 6 \\ 1 & 0 \end{bmatrix}$, then find the value of $a^2 + b^2$.

7. If $3A - B = \begin{bmatrix} 5 & 0 \\ 1 & 1 \end{bmatrix}$ and $B = \begin{bmatrix} 4 & 3 \\ 2 & 5 \end{bmatrix}$, then find matrix A .

8. If A is a square matrix such that $A^2 = A$, then what is the simplified value of $(I - A)^3 + A$?

9. If A is a square matrix such that $A^2 = A$, then what is the simplified of $(A - I)^3 + (A + I)^3 - 7A$?

10. If $\begin{bmatrix} 2 & 3 \\ 5 & 7 \end{bmatrix}\begin{bmatrix} 1 & -3 \\ -2 & 4 \end{bmatrix} = \begin{bmatrix} -4 & 6 \\ -9 & x \end{bmatrix}$, then find value of x.

11. If $\begin{bmatrix} 1 & 0 & 0 \\ 0 & y & 0 \\ 0 & 0 & 1 \end{bmatrix}\begin{bmatrix} x \\ -1 \\ z \end{bmatrix} = \begin{bmatrix} 1 \\ 2 \\ 1 \end{bmatrix}$, then find $x + y + z$.

12. For which value of x , $\begin{bmatrix} 1 & x & 1 \end{bmatrix} \begin{bmatrix} 1 & 2 & 3 \\ 4 & 5 & 6 \\ 3 & 2 & 5 \end{bmatrix} \begin{bmatrix} 1 \\ 2 \\ 3 \end{bmatrix} = [0]$?

13. If $\begin{bmatrix} 2x & 3 \end{bmatrix} \begin{bmatrix} 1 & 2 \\ -3 & 0 \end{bmatrix} \begin{bmatrix} x \\ 3 \end{bmatrix} = O$, then what is the value of x?

14. If $A = \begin{bmatrix} 0 & 0 \\ 2 & 0 \end{bmatrix}$, then find A^6.

15. If $A = \begin{bmatrix} 3 & -3 \\ -3 & 3 \end{bmatrix}$ and $A^2 = kA$, then find the value of k.

16. If $\begin{bmatrix} a+b & 2 \\ 5 & b \end{bmatrix} = \begin{bmatrix} 6 & 5 \\ 2 & 2 \end{bmatrix}^T$, then what is the value of a ?

17. If $\begin{bmatrix} 0 & 2b & -2 \\ 3 & 1 & 3 \\ 3a & 3 & -1 \end{bmatrix}$ is a symmetric matrix , then find the values of a and b.

18. If $\begin{bmatrix} 0 & a & -3 \\ 2 & 0 & -1 \\ b & 1 & 0 \end{bmatrix}$ is a skew-symmetric matrix , then find the values a and b.

ANSWERS

1. 81

2. 6

3. $\dfrac{9}{2}$

4. $x = -\dfrac{5}{3}$, $y = 7$

5. x = 4, y = 2, z = 0 or x = 2, y = 4, z = 0

6. 20

7. $\begin{bmatrix} 3 & 1 \\ 1 & 2 \end{bmatrix}$

8. I

9. A

10. 13

11. 0

12. $-\dfrac{9}{8}$

13. $0, -\dfrac{3}{2}$

14. $\begin{bmatrix} 0 & 0 \\ 0 & 0 \end{bmatrix}$

15. 6

16. 4

17. $-\dfrac{2}{3}, \dfrac{3}{2}$

18. $-2, 3$

LONG ANSWER TYPE QUESTIONS

1. If $A = \begin{bmatrix} 2 & 3 \\ -1 & 2 \end{bmatrix}$, then show that $A^2 - 4A + 7I = 0$. Hence find A^5.

2. Find the value of x if $\begin{bmatrix} 1 & x & 1 \end{bmatrix} \begin{bmatrix} 1 & 3 & 2 \\ 2 & 5 & 1 \\ 15 & 3 & 2 \end{bmatrix} \begin{bmatrix} 1 \\ 2 \\ x \end{bmatrix} = 0$

3. Let $A = \begin{bmatrix} -1 & -4 \\ 1 & 3 \end{bmatrix}$, prove that : $A^n = \begin{bmatrix} 1-2n & -4n \\ n & 1+2n \end{bmatrix}$.

19

4. Let $A = \begin{bmatrix} 0 & -\tan\dfrac{\alpha}{2} \\ \tan\dfrac{\alpha}{2} & 0 \end{bmatrix}$ and $I = \begin{bmatrix} 1 & 0 \\ 0 & 1 \end{bmatrix}$. Prove that $I + A = (I - A)\begin{bmatrix} \cos\alpha & -\sin\alpha \\ \sin\alpha & \cos\alpha \end{bmatrix}$.

5. Express $A = \begin{bmatrix} 2 & -2 & -4 \\ -1 & 3 & 4 \\ 1 & -2 & -3 \end{bmatrix}$ as the sum of a symmetric and a skew-symmetric matrix.

6. Show that $A = \begin{bmatrix} 2 & -3 \\ 3 & 4 \end{bmatrix}$ satisfies the equation $x^2 - 6x - 17 = 0$. Thus find A^{-1}.

7. If $A = \begin{bmatrix} 3 & 1 \\ 7 & 5 \end{bmatrix}$, find x and y such that $A^2 + xI = yA$. Hence find A^{-1}.

8. For the matrix $A = \begin{bmatrix} 3 & 2 \\ 1 & 1 \end{bmatrix}$, find the numbers a and b such that $A^2 + aA + bI = 0$. Hence, find A^{-1}.

9. Find the matrix P satisfying the matrix equation $\begin{bmatrix} 3 & 2 \\ 7 & 5 \end{bmatrix} P \begin{bmatrix} -1 & 1 \\ -1 & 1 \end{bmatrix} = \begin{bmatrix} 2 & -1 \\ 0 & 4 \end{bmatrix}$.

ANSWERS

1. $\begin{bmatrix} -118 & -93 \\ 31 & -118 \end{bmatrix}$

2. $x = -14$ or -2

5. $\begin{bmatrix} 2 & -3/2 & -3/2 \\ -3/2 & 3 & 1 \\ -3/2 & 1 & -3 \end{bmatrix} + \begin{bmatrix} 0 & -1/2 & -5/2 \\ 1/2 & 0 & 3 \\ 5/2 & -3 & 0 \end{bmatrix}$

6. $\dfrac{1}{17}\begin{bmatrix} 4 & 3 \\ -3 & 2 \end{bmatrix}$

7. $\begin{aligned} x &= 8 \\ y &= 8 \end{aligned}$, $A^{-1} = \begin{bmatrix} 5/8 & -1/8 \\ -7/8 & 3/8 \end{bmatrix}$

8. $\begin{aligned} a &= -4 \\ b &= 1 \end{aligned}$, $A^{-1} = \begin{bmatrix} 1 & -2 \\ -1 & 3 \end{bmatrix}$

9. $\begin{bmatrix} -16 & 3 \\ 24 & -5 \end{bmatrix}$

DETERMINANTS
SHORT ANSWER TYPE QUESTIONS

1. Let A be a square matrix of order 3×3 then find the value of $|4A|$.

2. If $x \in N$ and $\begin{vmatrix} x+3 & -2 \\ -3x & 2x \end{vmatrix} = 8$, then find the value of x.

3. If $\begin{vmatrix} 2 & 4 \\ 5 & 1 \end{vmatrix} = \begin{vmatrix} 2x & 4 \\ 6 & x \end{vmatrix}$, then find the value of x.

4. If $A = \begin{vmatrix} x & 2 \\ 2 & x \end{vmatrix}$ and $|A|^3 = 125$, then find x.

5. If A is a skew-symmetric matrix of order 3, then the value of $|A|$ is

6. If $\begin{vmatrix} 2 & 3 & 2 \\ x & x & x \\ 4 & 9 & 1 \end{vmatrix} + 3 = 0$, then find the value of x.

7. If A is a square matrix such that $|A| = 5$, then find the value of $|AA^T|$.

8. If area of triangle is 35 sq units with vertices $(2, -6)$, $(5, 4)$ and $(k, 4)$. Then find k.

9. If A_{ij} is the co-factor of the element a_{ij} of the determinant $\begin{vmatrix} 2 & -3 & 5 \\ 6 & 0 & 4 \\ 1 & 5 & -7 \end{vmatrix}$, the value of $a_{32} \cdot A_{32}$ is

10. If for any 2×2 square matrix A, $A(\text{adj } A) = \begin{bmatrix} 8 & 0 \\ 0 & 8 \end{bmatrix}$, then the value of $|A|$ is

11. If A is a square matrix of order 3 such that $|\text{adj}A| = 64$, then value of $|A|$ is

12. If A is a square matrix of order 3, with $|A| = 9$, then the value of $|2.\text{adj } A|$ is

13. If $A = \begin{vmatrix} 2 & k & -3 \\ 0 & 2 & 5 \\ 1 & 1 & 3 \end{vmatrix}$, then A^{-1} exists if

14. If A and B are matrices of order 3 and $|A| = 4$, $|B| = 5$, then find then value of $|3AB|$.

ANSWERS

1. $64|A|$ **2.** 2   **3.** $\pm\sqrt{3}$ **4.** ± 3

5. 0   **6.** -1 **7.** 25   **8.** 12, -2

9. 110   **10.** 8   **11.** ± 8 **12.** 648

13. $k \neq -\dfrac{8}{5}$ **14.** 60

LONG ANSWER TYPE QUESTIONS

1. Solve the following system of equations by matrix method:
$x + 2y + z = 7$, $x + 3z = 11$, $2x - 3y = 1$.

2. Solve the following system of equations by matrix method:
$$\frac{2}{x} + \frac{3}{y} + \frac{10}{z} = 4, \frac{4}{x} - \frac{6}{y} + \frac{5}{z} = 1, \frac{6}{x} + \frac{9}{y} - \frac{20}{z} = 2, x, y, z \neq 0$$

3. Find A^{-1}, where $A = \begin{bmatrix} 1 & 2 & 5 \\ 1 & -1 & -1 \\ 2 & 3 & -1 \end{bmatrix}$. Hence solve the equations $x + 2y + 5z = 10$, $x - y - z = -2$ and

$2x + 3y - z = -11$

4. Find A^{-1}, where $A = \begin{bmatrix} 1 & 1 & 1 \\ 1 & 2 & -3 \\ 2 & -1 & 3 \end{bmatrix}$. Hence solve

$\quad\quad x + y + 2z = 0$, $x + 2y - z = 9$ and $x - 3y + 3z = -14$

5. Find the matrix P satisfying the matrix equation : $\begin{bmatrix} 2 & 1 \\ 3 & 2 \end{bmatrix} P \begin{bmatrix} -3 & 2 \\ 5 & -3 \end{bmatrix} = \begin{bmatrix} 1 & 2 \\ 2 & -1 \end{bmatrix}$

6. Given that $A = \begin{bmatrix} 1 & -1 & 0 \\ 2 & 3 & 4 \\ 0 & 1 & 2 \end{bmatrix}$ and $B = \begin{bmatrix} 2 & 2 & -4 \\ -4 & 2 & -4 \\ 2 & -1 & 5 \end{bmatrix}$, find AB. Use this product to solve the

following system of equations: $x - y = 3$; $2x + 3y + 4z = 17$; $y + 2z = 7$.

ANSWERS

1. $A^{-1} = \dfrac{1}{18} \begin{bmatrix} 9 & -3 & 6 \\ 6 & -2 & -2 \\ -3 & 7 & -2 \end{bmatrix}$, $x = 2$, $y = 1$, $z = 3$.

2. $A^{-1} = \dfrac{1}{1200} \begin{bmatrix} 75 & 150 & 75 \\ 110 & -100 & 30 \\ 72 & 0 & -24 \end{bmatrix}$, $x = 2$, $y = 3$, $z = 5$.

3. $A^{-1} = \dfrac{1}{27} \begin{bmatrix} 4 & 17 & 3 \\ -1 & -11 & 6 \\ 5 & 1 & -3 \end{bmatrix}$, $x = -1$, $y = -2$, $z = 3$.

4. $A^{-1} = -\dfrac{1}{11} \begin{bmatrix} 3 & -4 & -5 \\ -9 & 1 & 4 \\ -5 & 3 & 1 \end{bmatrix}$, $x = 1$, $y = 3$, $z = -2$

5. $P = \begin{bmatrix} 25 & 15 \\ -37 & -22 \end{bmatrix}$

6. $x = 2$, $y = -1$ and $z = 4$

CONTINUITY & DIFFERENTIABILITY

* A function f is said to be continuous at x = a if

    Left hand limit = Right hand limit = value of the function at x = a

    i.e. $\lim\limits_{x \to a^-} f(x) = \lim\limits_{x \to a^+} f(x) = f(a)$

    i.e. $\lim\limits_{h \to 0} f(a-h) = \lim\limits_{h \to 0} f(a+h) = f(a)$.

* A function is said to be differentiable at x = a

    if $Lf'(a) = Rf'(a)$ i.e $\lim\limits_{h \to 0} \dfrac{f(a-h) - f(a)}{-h} = \lim\limits_{h \to 0} \dfrac{f(a+h) - f(a)}{h}$

(i) $\dfrac{d}{dx}(x^n) = n\, x^{n-1}, \quad \dfrac{d}{dx}\left(\dfrac{1}{x^n}\right) = -\dfrac{n}{x^{n+1}}, \quad \dfrac{d}{dx}\left(\sqrt{x}\right) = -\dfrac{1}{2\sqrt{x}}$

(ii) $\dfrac{d}{dx}(x) = 1$ (iii) $\dfrac{d}{dx}(c) = 0, \forall\, c \in R$

(iv) $\dfrac{d}{dx}(a^x) = a^x \log a, a > 0, a \neq 1.$ (v) $\dfrac{d}{dx}(e^x) = e^x.$

(vi) $\dfrac{d}{dx}(\log_a x) =, \dfrac{1}{x \log a} a > 0, a \neq 1, x$ (vii) $\dfrac{d}{dx}(\log x) = \dfrac{1}{x}, x > 0$

(viii) $\dfrac{d}{dx}(\log_a|x|) = \dfrac{1}{x \log a}, a > 0, a \neq 1, x \neq 0$ (ix) $\dfrac{d}{dx}(\log|x|) = \dfrac{1}{x}, x \neq 0$

(x) $\dfrac{d}{dx}(\sin x) = \cos x, \forall\, x \in R.$ (xi) $\dfrac{d}{dx}(\cos x) = -\sin x, \forall\, x \in R.$

(xii) $\dfrac{d}{dx}(\tan x) = \sec^2 x, \forall\, x \in R.$ (xiii) $\dfrac{d}{dx}(\cot x) = -\operatorname{cosec}^2 x, \forall\, x \in R.$

(xiv) $\dfrac{d}{dx}(\sec x) = \sec x \tan x, \forall\, x \in R.$ (xv) $\dfrac{d}{dx}(\operatorname{cosec} x) = -\operatorname{cosec} x \cot x, \forall\, x \in R.$

(xvi) $\dfrac{d}{dx}(\sin^{-1}x) = \dfrac{1}{\sqrt{1-x^2}}.$ (xvii) $\dfrac{d}{dx}(\cos^{-1}x) = \dfrac{-1}{\sqrt{1-x^2}}.$

(xviii) $\dfrac{d}{dx}(\tan^{-1}x) = \dfrac{1}{1+x^2}, \forall\, x \in R$ (xix) $\dfrac{d}{dx}(\cot^{-1}x) = -\dfrac{1}{1+x^2}, \forall\, x \in R.$

(xx) $\dfrac{d}{dx}(\sec^{-1}x) = \dfrac{1}{|x|\sqrt{x^2-1}}.$ (xxi) $\dfrac{d}{dx}(\operatorname{cosec}^{-1}x) = -\dfrac{1}{|x|\sqrt{x^2-1}}.$

(xxii) $\dfrac{d}{dx}(|x|) = \dfrac{x}{|x|}, x \neq 0$ (xxiii) $\dfrac{d}{dx}(ku) = k\dfrac{du}{dx}$

(xxiv) $\dfrac{d}{dx}(u \pm v) = \dfrac{du}{dx} \pm \dfrac{dv}{dx}$ (xxv) $\dfrac{d}{dx}(u.v) = u\dfrac{dv}{dx} + v\dfrac{du}{dx}$

(xxvi) $\dfrac{d}{dx}\left(\dfrac{u}{v}\right) = \dfrac{v\dfrac{du}{dx} - u\dfrac{dv}{dx}}{v^2}$

SOME ILUSTRATIONS :

**Q. If $f(x) = \begin{cases} 3ax + b, & \text{if } x > 1 \\ 11 & \text{if } x = 1 \\ 5ax - 2b, & \text{if } x < 1 \end{cases}$, continuous at x = 1, find the values of a and b.

23

Sol. $\lim_{x\to 1^-} f(x) = \lim_{x\to 1^+} f(x) = f(1)$.........(i)

$\lim_{x\to 1^-} f(x) = \lim_{h\to 0} f(1-h) = \lim_{h\to 0}[5a(1-h)-2b] = 5a-2b$

$\lim_{x\to 1^+} f(x) = \lim_{h\to 0} f(1+h) = \lim_{h\to 0}[3a(1+h)+b] = 3a+b$

$f(1) = 11$

From (i) $\quad 3a+b = 5a-2b = 11$ and solution is $a = 3$, $b = 2$

Q. Find the relationship between a and b so that the function defined by $f(x) = \begin{cases} ax+1 & \text{,if } x \le 3 \\ bx+3 & \text{,if } x > 3 \end{cases}$

is continuous at $x = 3$.

Sol. $\because f(x)$ is cont. at $x = 3 \Rightarrow \lim_{x\to 3^-} f(x) = \lim_{x\to 3^+} f(x) = f(3)$.........(i)

$\lim_{x\to 3^-} f(x) = \lim_{h\to 0} f(3-h) = \lim_{h\to 0}[a(3-h)+1] = 3a+1$

$\lim_{x\to 3^+} f(x) = \lim_{h\to 0} f(3+h) = \lim_{h\to 0}[b(3+h)+3] = 3b+3$

$f(3) = 3a+1$

From (i) $\quad 3a+1 = 3b+3 = 3a+1 \Rightarrow 3a+1 = 3b+3$

$\Rightarrow$ **$3a-3b = 2$** is the required relation between a and b

If $y = (\log_e x)^x + x^{\log_e x}$ find $\dfrac{dy}{dx}$.

Sol. $y = (\log_e x)^x + x^{\log_e x} = e^{\log\{(\log_e x)^x\}} + e^{\log\{x^{\log_e x}\}}$

$= e^{x\log\{(\log_e x)\}} + e^{\log_e x . \log_e x}$

$\dfrac{dy}{dx}. = e^{x\log\{(\log_e x)\}}\left[x.\dfrac{1}{\log x}.\dfrac{1}{x} + \log(\log x).1\right] + e^{\log_e x.\log_e x}\left[\dfrac{\log x}{x} + \dfrac{\log x}{x}\right]$

$= (\log_e x)^x\left[\dfrac{1}{\log x} + \log(\log x)\right] + x^{\log_e x}\left[2\dfrac{\log x}{x}\right]$

If $x = a(\theta - \sin\theta)$, $y = a(1+\cos\theta)$, find $\dfrac{d^2 y}{dx^2}$ at $\theta = \dfrac{\pi}{2}$

Sol. $x = a(\theta - \sin\theta) \Rightarrow \dfrac{dx}{d\theta} = a(1-\cos\theta)$

$y = a(1+\cos\theta) \qquad \Rightarrow \dfrac{dy}{d\theta} = a(-\sin\theta)$

$\dfrac{dy}{dx} = \dfrac{dy/d\theta}{dx/d\theta} = \dfrac{a(-\sin\theta)}{a(1-\cos\theta)} = -\dfrac{2\sin\theta/2.\cos\theta s\theta}{2\sin^2\theta/2} = -\cot\dfrac{\theta}{2}$

$\dfrac{d^2 y}{dx^2} = \text{cosec}^2\dfrac{\theta}{2}.\dfrac{1}{2}.\dfrac{d\theta}{dx} = \dfrac{1}{2}\text{cosec}^2\dfrac{\theta}{2}.\dfrac{1}{a(1-\cos\theta)}$

$\left(\dfrac{d^2 y}{dx^2}\right)_{\theta=\frac{\pi}{2}} = \dfrac{1}{2}\text{cosec}^2\dfrac{\pi}{4}.\dfrac{1}{a\left(1-\cos\dfrac{\pi}{2}\right)} = \dfrac{1}{2}.2.\dfrac{1}{a} = \dfrac{1}{a}$

24

** If $y = \sin(m\sin^{-1} x)$, prove that $(1-x^2)\dfrac{d^2y}{dx^2} - x\dfrac{dy}{dx} + m^2y = 0$

Sol. $y = \sin(m\sin^{-1} x) \Rightarrow \dfrac{dy}{dx} = \cos(m\sin^{-1} x).\dfrac{m}{\sqrt{1-x^2}}$

$\Rightarrow \sqrt{1-x^2}\,\dfrac{dy}{dx} = m\cos(m\sin^{-1} x)$

Again diff.w.r.t.x, $\sqrt{1-x^2}\dfrac{d^2y}{dx^2} + \dfrac{dy}{dx}\left(\dfrac{-2x}{\sqrt{1-x^2}}\right) = -m\sin(m\sin^{-1} x).\dfrac{m}{\sqrt{1-x^2}}$

$\Rightarrow (1-x^2)\dfrac{d^2y}{dx^2} - x\dfrac{dy}{dx} = -m^2\sin(m\sin^{-1} x) = -m^2y$

$\Rightarrow (1-x^2)\dfrac{d^2y}{dx^2} - x\dfrac{dy}{dx} + m^2y = 0$

SHORT ANSWER TYPE QUESTIONS

1. Discuss the continuity of the function $f(x) = \begin{cases} 2x-3, & \text{if } x < 2 \\ 5x-9, & \text{if } x \geq 2 \end{cases}$.

2. Discuss the continuity of the greatest integer function $f(x) = [x]$ at integral points.

3. Discuss the continuity of the identity function $f(x) = x$.

4. Discuss the continuity of a polynomial function.

5. Find the points of discontinuity of the function f defined by $f(x) = \begin{cases} 3, & \text{if } 0 \leq x \leq 1 \\ 4, & \text{if } 1 < x < 3 \\ 5, & \text{if } 3 \leq x \leq 10 \end{cases}$

6. Find the number of points at which the function $f(x) = \dfrac{9-x^2}{9x-x^3}$ is discontinuous.

7. Discuss the continuity of $f(x) = \begin{cases} x^{10} - 1, & \text{if } x \leq 1 \\ x^2, & \text{if } x > 1 \end{cases}$, at $x = 1$.

8. Discuss the continuity of modulus function $f(x) = |x - 2|$.

9. Discuss the continuity of the function $f(x)$ is defined as $f(x) = \begin{cases} \dfrac{x}{\sqrt{x^2}}, & \text{if } x \neq 0 \\ 0, & \text{if } x = 0 \end{cases}$ at $x = 0$.

10. Find the value of k for which $f(x) = \begin{cases} \dfrac{\sin 2x}{5x}, & x \neq 0 \\ k, & x = 0 \end{cases}$ is continuous at $x = 0$.

11. Discuss the continuity of the function $f(x) = \begin{cases} \dfrac{x}{\sqrt{x^2}}, & \text{if } x \neq 0 \\ 0, & \text{if } x = 0 \end{cases}$ at $x = 0$.

12. Find the value of k for which $f(x) = \begin{cases} \dfrac{1-\cos 4x}{2x^2}, & x \neq 0 \\ k, & x = 0 \end{cases}$ is continuous at $x = 0$.

13. The value of k for which $f(x) = \begin{cases} \dfrac{kx}{|x|}, & \text{if } x < 0 \\ 3, & \text{if } x \geq 0 \end{cases}$ is continuous at x = 0 is :

14. Discuss the differentiability of the greatest integer function defined by $f(x) = [x]$, $0 < x < 3$ at x = 1.

15. Discuss the differentiability of the function $f(x) = |x - 2|$ at x = 2.

16. Find : $\dfrac{d}{dx}\left[\sin^2\left(\sqrt{\cos x}\right)\right]$

17. Find : $\dfrac{d}{dx}\left[\log\sin\sqrt{x^2+1}\right]$

18. Find : $\dfrac{d}{dx}\left[2^{-x}\right]$

19. Find : $\dfrac{d}{dx}\left[e^{1+\log_e x}\right]$

20. Find : $\dfrac{d}{dx}\left[2^{\cos^2 x}\right]$

21. Find : $\dfrac{d}{dx}\left[\log_e\tan\left(\dfrac{\pi}{4}+\dfrac{x}{2}\right)\right]$

22. Find : $\dfrac{d}{dx}\left[\tan^{-1}\left(\dfrac{\sqrt{1+x^2}-1}{x}\right)\right]$

23. Find : $\dfrac{d}{dx}\left[\sin^{-1}\left(\dfrac{1}{\sqrt{1+x^2}}\right)\right]$

24. Find : $\dfrac{d}{dx}\left[\tan^{-1}\left(\sqrt{\dfrac{1+\sin x}{1-\sin x}}\right)\right]$, where $0 < x < \dfrac{\pi}{4}$

25. Find : $\dfrac{d}{dx}\left[\sin^{-1}\left(\dfrac{\sin x+\cos x}{\sqrt{2}}\right)\right]$

26. Find : $\dfrac{d}{dx}\left[x^{\sin x}\right]$

27. Find : $\dfrac{d}{dx}\left[x^{x^x}\right]$

ANSWERS

1. Continuous for all real values of x
2. Continuous everywhere
3. Continuous everywhere
4. Continuous everywhere
5. 1, 3
6. Exactly at two points
7. Continuous at x = 1
8. Continuous everywhere
9. Discontinuous at x = 0
10. $\dfrac{2}{5}$
11. Discontinuous at x = 0
12. 4
13. k = −3
14. not differentiable at x = 1
15. not differentiable at x = 2
16. $-\dfrac{2\sin x.\sin(\sqrt{\cos x}).\cos(\sqrt{\cos x})}{2(\sqrt{\cos x})}$
17. $\dfrac{x\cos\sqrt{x^2+1}}{\sqrt{x^2+1}.\sin\sqrt{x^2+1}}$
18. $-\dfrac{1}{2^x}\log 2$
19. e
20. $-2^{\cos^2 x}.\log 2.\sin 2x$
21. sec x
22. $\dfrac{1}{2(1+x^2)}$
23. $-\dfrac{1}{1+x^2}$
24. $\dfrac{1}{2}$
25. 1
26. $x^{\sin x}\left(\cos x.\log_e x+\dfrac{\sin x}{x}\right)$
27. $x^{x^x}.x^x\left[(1+\log x)\log x+\dfrac{1}{x}\right]$

LONG ANSWER TYPE QUESTIONS

1. Find the value of k for which $f(x) = \begin{cases} \dfrac{\sqrt{1+kx} - \sqrt{1-kx}}{x} &, -1 \le x < 0 \\ \dfrac{2x+1}{x-1} &, 0 \le x \le 1 \end{cases}$ is continuous at x = 0.

2. Find the value of k for which $f(x) = \begin{cases} \dfrac{\sqrt{1+kx} - \sqrt{1-kx}}{x} &, -1 \le x < 0 \\ \dfrac{2x+1}{x-1} &, 0 \le x \le 1 \end{cases}$ is continuous at x = 0 .

3. Find the value of k for which $f(x) = \begin{cases} \dfrac{(x+3)^2 - 36}{x-3} &, \text{if } x \ne 0 \\ k &, \text{if } x = 0 \end{cases}$ is continuous at x = 3 .

4. Find the value of k for which $f(x) = \begin{cases} kx+1, & \text{if } x \le \pi \\ \cos x &, \text{if } x > \pi \end{cases}$ is continuous at x = π .

5. Find the value of k for which $f(x) = \begin{cases} \dfrac{\sin 5x}{x^2 + 2x}, & \text{if } x \ne 0 \\ k+1 &, \text{if } x = 0 \end{cases}$ is continuous at x = 0 .

6. If $f(x) = \begin{cases} 3ax+b, & \text{if } x > 1 \\ 11 & \text{if } x = 1 \\ 5ax-2b, & \text{if } x < 1 \end{cases}$, continuous at x = 1, find the values of a and b.

7. Determine a, b, c so that $f(x) = \begin{cases} \dfrac{\sin(a+1)x + \sin x}{x}, & x < 0 \\ c &, x = 0 \\ \dfrac{\sqrt{x + bx^2} - \sqrt{x}}{bx^{3/2}}, & x > 0 \end{cases}$ is continuous at x = 0.

8. If $f(x) = \begin{cases} \dfrac{k \cos x}{\pi - 2x}, & x \ne \dfrac{\pi}{2} \\ 3 &, x = \dfrac{\pi}{2} \end{cases}$, is continuous at $x = \frac{\pi}{2}$, find k.

9. Show that the function f defined by $f(x) = \begin{cases} 3x-2 &, 0 < x \le 1 \\ 2x^2 - x &, 1 < x \le 2 \\ 5x-4 &, x > 2 \end{cases}$ is continuous at x = 2 but not differentiable .

10. Find the relationship between a and b so that the function defined by

$$f(x) = \begin{cases} ax+1 &, \text{if } x \le 3 \\ bx+3 &, \text{if } x > 3 \end{cases}$$ is continuous at x = 3.

11. For what value of λ the function $f(x) = \begin{cases} \lambda(x^2 - 2x) &, \text{if } x \le 0 \\ 4x+1 &, \text{if } x > 0 \end{cases}$ is continuous at x = 0.

12. If $f(x) = \begin{cases} \dfrac{x-4}{|x-4|} + a, & \text{if } x < 4 \\ a+b & \text{if } x = 4 \\ \dfrac{x-4}{|x-4|} + b & \text{if } x > 4 \end{cases}$ is continuous at $x = 4$, find a, b.

13. If the function $f(x) = \begin{cases} x^2 + ax + b, & \text{if } 0 \le x < 2 \\ 3x + 2, & \text{if } 2 \le x \le 4 \\ 2ax + 5b, & \text{if } 4 < x \le 8 \end{cases}$ is continuous on $[0\,,\,8]$, find the value of a & b.

14. If $f(x) = \begin{cases} \dfrac{1 - \sin^3 x}{3\cos^2 x}, & \text{if } x < \dfrac{\pi}{2} \\ a & \text{if } x = \dfrac{\pi}{2} \\ \dfrac{b(1 - \sin x)}{(\pi - 2x)^2} & \text{if } x > \dfrac{\pi}{2} \end{cases}$ is continuous at $x = \dfrac{\pi}{2}$, find a, b.

15. Discuss the continuity of $f(x) = |x - 1| + |x - 2|$ at $x = 1$ & $x = 2$.

16. If $y = \left(\log_e x\right)^x + x^{\log_e x}$ find $\dfrac{dy}{dx}$.

17. If $x = a(\theta - \sin\theta)$, $y = a(1 + \cos\theta)$, find $\dfrac{d^2y}{dx^2}$ at $\theta = \dfrac{\pi}{2}$

18. If $x = a\left(\cos\theta + \log\tan\dfrac{\theta}{2}\right)$ and $y = a\sin\theta$ find $\dfrac{dy}{dx}$ at $\theta = \dfrac{\pi}{4}$.

19. If $y = \sin(m\sin^{-1} x)$, prove that $\left(1 - x^2\right)\dfrac{d^2y}{dx^2} - x\dfrac{dy}{dx} + m^2 y = 0$

20. If $x = \sqrt{a^{\sin^{-1} t}}$, $y = \sqrt{a^{\cos^{-1} t}}$, show that $\dfrac{dy}{dx} = -\dfrac{y}{x}$.

21. If $y = \left(x + \sqrt{x^2 + a^2}\right)^n$, prove that $\dfrac{dy}{dx} = \dfrac{ny}{\sqrt{x^2 + a^2}}$

22. If $\log_e \sqrt{x^2 + y^2} = \tan^{-1}\left(\dfrac{y}{x}\right)$, prove that $\dfrac{dy}{dx} = \dfrac{x+y}{x-y}$.

23. If $x^m \cdot y^n = (x+y)^{m+n}$, prove that $\dfrac{dy}{dx} = \dfrac{y}{x}$

24. If $x\sqrt{1+y} + y\sqrt{1+x} = 0$, $-1 < x < 1$, prove that $\dfrac{dy}{dx} = -\dfrac{1}{(1+x)^2}$

25. If $\sqrt{1-x^2} + \sqrt{1-y^2} = a(x-y)$, show that $\dfrac{dy}{dx} = \sqrt{\dfrac{1-y^2}{1-x^2}}$

26. If $y = \sqrt{x^2 + 1} - \log\left(\dfrac{1}{x} + \sqrt{1 + \dfrac{1}{x^2}}\right)$, find $\dfrac{dy}{dx}$.

27. If $x = \alpha\sin 2t(1 + \cos 2t)$ and $y = \beta\cos 2t(1 - \cos 2t)$, show that $\dfrac{dy}{dx} = \dfrac{\beta}{\alpha}\tan t$.

28. If $y = \sqrt{x+1} - \sqrt{x-1}$, prove that $(x^2 - 1)\dfrac{d^2y}{dx^2} + x\dfrac{dy}{dx} - \dfrac{1}{4}y = 0$

29. If $y = \sqrt{x + \sqrt{x + \sqrt{x + \dots \infty}}}$, then find $\dfrac{dy}{dx}$.

30. If $(\cos x)^y = (\sin y)^x$, then find $\dfrac{dy}{dx}$.

LONG ANSWER TYPE QUESTIONS
ANSWERS

1. $k = -\dfrac{1}{2}$

2. $k = -1$

3. $k = 12$

4. $k = -\dfrac{2}{\pi}$

5. $k = \dfrac{3}{2}$

6. $a = 3, b = 2$

7. $a = -3/2, c = 1/2$, b is any non-zero real number

8. $k = 6$

10. $\mathbf{3a - 3b = 2}$ is the relation between a and b

11. there is no value of λ for which f(x) is contonuous at 0.

12. $a = 1, b = -1$

13. $a = 3, b = -2$

14. $a = \dfrac{1}{2}, b = 4$

15. continuous at $x = 1$ & $x = 2$.

16. $(\log x)^x \left[\dfrac{1}{\log x} + \log(\log x) \right] + x^{\log x} \left[2 \dfrac{\log x}{x} \right]$

17. $\dfrac{1}{a}$

18. 1

26. $\dfrac{\sqrt{x^2 + 1}}{x}$

29. $\dfrac{1}{2y - 1}$

30. $\dfrac{\log \sin y + y \tan x}{(\log \cos x - x \cot y)}$

APPLICATION OF DERIVATIVE

** Whenever one quantity y varies with another quantity x, satisfying some rule $y = f(x)$, then $\dfrac{dy}{dx}$ (or f

'(x)) represents the rate of change of y with respect to x and $\left[\dfrac{dy}{dx}\right]_{x=x_0}$ (or $f'(x_0)$) represents the rate of

change of y with respect to x at $x = x_0$.

** Let I be an open interval contained in the domain of a real valued function f. Then f is said to be

(i) **increasing on I** if $x_1 < x_2$ in $I \Rightarrow f(x_1) \leq f(x_2)$ for all $x_1, x_2 \in I$.

(ii) **strictly increasing on I** if $x_1 < x_2$ in $I \Rightarrow f(x_1) < f(x_2)$ for all $x_1, x_2 \in I$.

(iii) **decreasing** on I if $x_1 < x_2$ in $I \Rightarrow f(x_1) \geq f(x_2)$ for all $x_1, x_2 \in I$.

(iv) **strictly decreasing** on I if $x_1 < x_2$ in $I \Rightarrow f(x_1) > f(x_2)$ for all $x_1, x_2 \in I$.

** (i) f is **strictly increasing in (a, b)** if $f'(x) > 0$ for each $x \in (a, b)$

　(ii) f is **strictly decreasing in (a, b)** if $f'(x) < 0$ for each $x \in (a, b)$

　(iii) A function will be increasing (decreasing) in **R** if it is so in every interval of **R**.

** Slope of the tangent to the curve $y = f(x)$ at the point (x_0, y_0) is given by $\left[\dfrac{dy}{dx}\right]_{(x_0, y_0)}$ $\left(= f'(x_0)\right)$.

** The **equation of the tangent at (x_0, y_0)** to the curve $y = f(x)$ is given by $y - y_0 = f'(x_0)(x - x_0)$.

** Slope of the normal to the curve $y = f(x)$ at (x_0, y_0) is $-\dfrac{1}{f'(x_0)}$.

** The **equation of the normal at (x_0, y_0)** to the curve $y = f(x)$ is given by $y - y_0 = -\dfrac{1}{f'(x_0)}(x - x_0)$.

** If slope of the tangent line is zero, then $\tan\theta = 0$ and so $\theta = 0$ which means the tangent line is parallel to the x-axis. In this case, the equation of the tangent at the point (x_0, y_0) is given by $y = y_0$.

** If $\theta \to \dfrac{\pi}{2}$, then $\tan\theta \to \infty$, which means the tangent line is perpendicular to the x-axis, i.e., parallel to

the y-axis. In this case, the equation of the tangent at (x_0, y_0) is given by $x = x_0$.

** Let f be a function defined on an interval I. Then

(a) f is said to have a maximum value in I, if there exists a point c in I such that

$f(c) \geq f(x)$, for all $x \in I$.

　　The number $f(c)$ is called the maximum value of f in I and the point c is called a point of maximum value of f in I.

　(b) f is said to have a minimum value in I, if there exists a point c in I such that

$f(c) \leq f(x)$, for all $x \in I$.

　　The number $f(c)$, in this case, is called the minimum value of f in I and the point c, in this case, is called a point of minimum value of f in I.

　(c) f is said to have an extreme value in I if there exists a point c in I such that $f(c)$ is either a maximum value or a minimum value of f in I.

　　The number $f(c)$, in this case, is called an extreme value of f in I and the point c is called an extreme point.

** **Absolute maxima and minima**

　　Let f be a function defined on the interval I and $c \in I$. Then

　(a) f(c) is absolute minimum if $f(x) \square \geq f(c)$ for all $x \in I$.

　(b) f(c) is absolute maximum if $f(x) \leq f(c)$ for all $x \in I$.

　(c) $c \in I$ is called the critical point off if $f'(c) = 0$

(d) Absolute maximum or minimum value of a continuous function f on [a, b] occurs at a or b or at critical points off (i.e. at the points where f 'is zero)

If $c_1, c_2, \ldots, c_n$ are the critical points lying in [a , b],

then absolute maximum value of f = max{f(a), f(c_1), f(c_2), \ldots, f(c_n), f(b)}

and absolute minimum value of f = min{f(a), f(c_1), f(c_2), \ldots, f(c_n), f(b)}.

** Local maxima and minima

(a)A function f is said to have a local maxima or simply a maximum value at x a if f(a ± h) ≤ f(a) for sufficiently small h

(b)A function f is said to have a local minima or simply a minimum value at x = a if f(a ± h) ≥ f(a).

** First derivative test : A function f has a maximum at a point x = a if

(i) f '(a) = 0, and

(ii) f '(x) changes sign from + ve to –ve in the neighbourhood of 'a' (points taken from left to right). However, f has a minimum at x = a, if

(i) f '(a) = 0, and

(ii) f '(x) changes sign from –ve to +ve in the neighbourhood of 'a'.

If f '(a) = 0 and f ' (x) does not change sign, then f(x) has neither maximum nor minimum and the point 'a' is called point of inflation.

The points where f '(x) = 0 are called stationary or critical points. The stationary points at which the function attains either maximum or minimum values are called extreme points.

** Second derivative test

(i) a function has a maxima at x = a if f '(x) 3. 4. b = 0 and f '' (a) <0

(ii) a function has a minima at x = a if f '(x) = 0 and f ''(a) > 0.

SOME ILUSTRATIONS :

Q. Find the rate of change of the volume of a sphere with respect to its surface area when the radius is 2 cm.

Sol. Radius of sphere(r) = 2cm

$$V = \frac{4}{3}\pi r^2 , \quad \frac{dV}{dr} = 4\pi r^2$$

$$A = 4\pi r^2 , \quad \frac{dA}{dr} = 8\pi r^2$$

$$\frac{dV}{dA} = \frac{dV/dr}{dA/dr} = \frac{4\pi r^2}{8\pi r} = \frac{r}{2}$$

$$\therefore \left(\frac{dV}{dA}\right)_{at\ r=2} = \frac{2}{2} = 1\ cm$$

Q. A ladder 5 m long is leaning against a wall. The bottom of the ladder is pulled along the ground, away from the wall, at the rate of 2 cm/s. How fast is its height on the wall decreasing when the foot of the ladder is 4 m away from the wall?

Sol. Given $\frac{dx}{dt} = 2\ cm/sec$

$$x^2 + y^2 = 25$$

when $x = 4, 16 + y^2 = 25 \Rightarrow y = 3$

Also $2x\frac{dx}{dt} + 2y\frac{dy}{dt} = 0$

$$\Rightarrow 2x \times 2 + 2y\frac{dy}{dt} = 0 \quad \Rightarrow \frac{dy}{dt} = -\frac{2x}{y} = \frac{-8}{3}$$

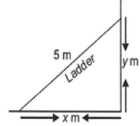

$\therefore$ rate of decrease of height on the wall $= \dfrac{8}{3}$ cm/sec.

Q. Find the intervals in which the function $f(x) = 5 + 36x + 3x^2 - 2x^3$ is increasing or decreasing.

Sol. $f(x) = 5 + 36x + 3x^2 - 2x^3$

$f'(x) = 36 + 6x - 6x^2 = 6(6 + x - x^2)$

$\qquad = -6(x - 3)(x + 2)$

$f'(x) = 0 \Rightarrow x = -2, 3$

$$\overset{\displaystyle \quad -\infty \qquad - \qquad -2 \qquad + \qquad 3 \qquad - \qquad \infty}{\longleftrightarrow}$$

$\therefore f(x)$ is increasing on $x \in (-2, 3)$ and $f(x)$ is decreasing on interval $x \in (-\infty, -2) \cup (3, \infty)$.

Q. Show that the semi-vertical angle of the cone of the maximum volume and of given slant height is $\tan\tan^{-1}(\sqrt{2})$.

Sol. Given $l^2 = r^2 + h^2$ \qquad\qquad ...(i)

$V = \dfrac{1}{3}\pi r^2 h = \dfrac{1}{3}\pi(l^2 - h^2)h = \dfrac{1}{3}\pi(l^2 h - h^3)$

$\dfrac{dV}{dh} = \dfrac{1}{3}\pi(l^2 - 3h^2)$

For Max. volume $\dfrac{dV}{dh} = 0 \Rightarrow \dfrac{1}{3}\pi(l^2 - 3h^2) = 0 \Rightarrow h = \dfrac{1}{\sqrt{3}}$

$\dfrac{d^2V}{dh^2} = \dfrac{1}{3}\pi(-6h) < 0 , \forall h$

$\therefore V$ is max. when $h = 1/\sqrt{3}$

From (i) $3h^3 = r^2 + h^2 \Rightarrow r^2 = 2h^2 \Rightarrow r = \sqrt{2}h$

In $\triangle OAB$ $\tan\alpha = \dfrac{r}{h} = \dfrac{\sqrt{2}h}{h} = \sqrt{2} \Rightarrow \alpha = \tan^{-1}\sqrt{2}$

Q. Prove that the volume of the largest cone that can be inscribed in a sphere of radius R is $\dfrac{8}{27}$ of the volume of the sphere.

Sol. In $\triangle OLC$

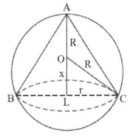

$R^2 = x^2 + r^2$ \qquad\qquad (i)

$V = \dfrac{1}{3}\pi r^2 h = \dfrac{1}{3}\pi r^2(R + x)$

$\quad = \dfrac{1}{3}\pi(R^2 - x^2)(R + x)$

$\quad = \dfrac{1}{3}\pi(R^3 + R^2 x - Rx^2 - x^3)$

$\dfrac{dV}{dx} = \dfrac{1}{3}\pi(R^2 - 2Rx - 3x^2) = \dfrac{1}{3}\pi(R^2 - 3Rx + Rx - 3x^2)$

$\quad = \dfrac{1}{3}\pi(R - 3x)(R + x)$

For max. volume $\dfrac{dV}{dx} = 0 \Rightarrow \dfrac{1}{3}\pi(R - 3x)(R + x)$

$$\Rightarrow (R - 3x) = 0 \text{ as } R + x \neq 0 \qquad \Rightarrow x = \frac{R}{3}$$

$$\frac{d^2V}{dx^2} = \frac{1}{3}\pi(-2R - 6x) = \frac{1}{3}\pi\left(-2R - 6\frac{R}{3}\right) = -\frac{4}{3}\pi R < 0$$

$$\therefore V \text{ is max. when } x = \frac{R}{3}$$

$$V = \frac{1}{3}\pi(R^2 - x^2)(R + x) = \frac{1}{3}\pi\left(R^2 - \frac{R^2}{9}\right)\left(R + \frac{R}{3}\right)$$

$$= \frac{1}{3}\pi . \frac{8}{9}R^2 . \frac{4}{3}R = \frac{8}{27}\left(\frac{4}{3}\pi R^3\right) = \frac{8}{27}. \text{Volume of the Sphere}$$

RATE OF CHANGE OF BODIES

SHORT ANSWER TYPE QUESTIONS

1. The side of a square is increasing at the rate of 0.2 cm/s. Find the rate of increase of the perimeter of the square.

2. The radius of a circle is increasing uniformly at the rate of 0.3 centimetre per second. At what rate is the area increasing when the radius is 10 cm? (Take $\pi = 3.14$.)

3. A balloon which always remains spherical, is being inflated by pumping in 900 cubic centimetres of gas per second. Find the rate at which the radius of the balloon is increasing when the radius is 15 cm.

4. A man 2 metres high walks at a uniform speed of 5 km/hr away from a lamp-post 6 metres high. Find the rate at which the length of his shadow increases.

5. A stone is dropped into a quiet lake and waves move in circles at a speed of 4 cm/sec. At the instant when the radius of the circular wave is 10 cm, how fast is the enclosed area increasing?

6. A particle moves along the curve $y = x^2 + 2x$. At what point(s) on the curve are the x and y coordinates of the particle changing at the same rate?

7. The bottom of a rectangular swimming tank is 25 m by 40 m. Water is pumped into the tank at the rate of 500 cubic metres per minute. Find the rate at which the level of water in the tank is rising.

8. A spherical ball of salt is dissolving in water in such a manner that the rate of decrease of the volume at any instant is proportional to the surface. Prove that the radius is decreasing at a constant rate.

9. A particle moves along the curve $y = x^3$. Find the points on the curve at which the y-coordinate changes three times more rapidly than the x-coordinate.

10. Find the point on the curve $y^2 = 8x$ for which the abscissa and ordinate change at the same rate?

11. Find an angle x which increases twice as fast as its sine.

12. The sides of an equilateral triangle are increasing at the rate of 2 cm/sec. Find the rate at which the area is increasing when the side is 10 cm.

13. The total revenue received from the sale of x units of a product is given by $R(x) = 10x^2 + 13x + 24$ Find the marginal revenue when $x = 5$, where by marginal revenue we mean the rate of change of total revenue w.r. to the number of items sold at an instant.

14. The total cost associated with the production of x units of an item is given by $C(x) = 0.007x^3 - 0.003x^2 + 15x + 4000$. Find the marginal cost when 17 units are produced, where by marginal cost we mean the instantaneous rate of change of the total cost at any level of output.

ANSWERS

1. 0.8 cm/sec

2. 18.84 cm^2/sec

3. $\frac{1}{\pi}$ cm/sec

4. $\dfrac{5}{2}$ km/hr   **5.** 80π cm^2/s   **6.** $\left(-\dfrac{1}{2}, -\dfrac{3}{4}\right)$

7. 0.5 m/minute   **9.** (1 , 1) and (–1 , –1)   **10.** (2 , 4)

11. $\dfrac{\pi}{3}$ **12.** $10\sqrt{3}$ cm^2/sec   **13.** ₹ 113

14. ₹20.967   **15.16.**

LONG ANSWER TYPE QUESTIONS

1. The length x of a rectangle is decreasing at the rate of 5 cm/minute and the width y is increasing at the rate of 4cm/minute. When x = 8 cm and y = 6 cm, find the rate of change of (a) the perimeter, (b) the area of the rectangle.

2. The volume of metal in a hollow sphere is constant. If the inner radius is increasing at the rate of 1 cm/sec, find the rate of increase of the outer radius when the radii are 4 cm and 8 cm respectively.

3. A kite is moving horizontally at a height of 151.5 meters. If the speed of kite is 10m/sec, how fast is the string being let out; when the kite is 250 m away from the boy who is flying the kite? The height of boy is 1.5 m.

4. Sand is pouring from a pipe at the rate of 12 cm^3/s. The falling sand forms a cone on the ground in such a way that the height of the cone is always one-sixth of the radius of the base.
How fast is the height of the sand cone increasing when the height is 4 cm?

5. A water tank has the shape of an inverted right circular cone with its axis vertical and vertex lower most. Its semi vertical angle is tan^{-1} (0.5) water is poured into it at a constant rate of 5cm^3/hr. Find the rate at which the level of the water is rising at the instant when the depth of water in the tank is 4m.

6. The top of a ladder 6 meters long is resting against a vertical wall on a level pavement, when the ladder begins to slide outwards. At the moment when the foot of the ladder is 4 meters from the wall, it is sliding away from the wall at the rate of 0.5 m/sec.
(a) How fast is the top-sliding downwards at this instance?
(b) How far is the foot from the wall when it and the top are moving at the same rate?

7. The two equal sides of an isosceles triangle with fixed base b are decreasing at the rate of 3 cm per second. How fast is the area decreasing when the two equal sides are equal to the base ?

8. Water is leaking from a conical funnel at the rate of 5 cm /s. If the radius of the base of funnel is 5 cm and height 10 cm, find the rate at which the water level is dropping when it is 2.5 cm from the top.

9. A man is moving away from a tower 41.6 m high at the rate of 2 m/s. Find the rate at which the angle of elevation of the top of tower is changing when he is at a distance of 30 m from the foot of the tower. Assume that the eye level of the man is 1.6 m from the ground.

10. Two men A and B start with velocities v at the same time from the junction of two roads inclined at 45° to each other. If they travel by different roads, find the rate at which they are being separated.

ANSWERS

1. (a)↓ @ 2 cm/ minute (b) ↑ @ 2 cm^2/ minute   **2.** $\dfrac{1}{4}$ cm/sec

3. 8 m/s.   **4.** $\dfrac{1}{48\pi}$ cm/sec   **5.** $\dfrac{35}{88}$ m/h

6. (a) $\dfrac{1}{\sqrt{5}}$ m/sec (b) $3\sqrt{2}$m   **7.** $\sqrt{3}$ bcm^2/sec   **8.** $\dfrac{16}{45\pi}$ cm/sec

9. $\dfrac{4}{25}$ radian/sec   **10.** $\sqrt{2-\sqrt{2}}$ v unit/s

34

INCREASING AND DECREASING FUNCTIONS
SHORT ANSWER TYPE QUESTIONS

1. If I be an open interval contained in the domain of a real valued function f and if $x_1 < x_2$ in I, then write the condition for which f is strictly increasing on I.

2. Show that the function given by f(x) = 4x + 3, x $\in$ R is strictly increasing on **R**.

3. Prove that the function f(x) = $\log_a(x)$ is increasing on $(0, \infty)$ if a>1 and decreasing on $(0, \infty)$ if 0 <a <1.

4. Show that the function f (x) = $x^2 - x + 1$ is neither increasing nor decreasing in (– 1, 1).

5. Find the least value of a such that the function f given by f (x) = $x^2 + ax + 1$ is strictly increasing on (1, 2) .

6. Show that the function given by f (x) = $x^3 - 3x^2 + 3x - 100$ is increasing in **R**.

7. Show that f(x) = $\dfrac{1}{1+x^2}$ decreases in the interval $[0, \infty]$ and increases in the interval $[-\infty, 0]$.

8. Find the interval in which y = $x^2 e^{-x}$ is increasing.

9. Show that the function f(x) = log(cos x) is strictly decreasing on $\left(0, \dfrac{\pi}{2}\right)$

10. Show that the function f(x) = $\cot^{-1} x + x$ increases in $(-\infty, \infty)$.

ANSWERS

1. if $f(x_1) \le f(x_2)$ for all $x_1, x_2 \in I$ 5. a = – 2   8. (0, 2)

LONG ANSWER TYPE QUESTIONS

1. Find the intervals in which the function f(x) = $4x^3 - 6x^2 - 72x + 30$ s strictly increasing or decreasing.

2. Find the intervals in which the function f(x) = $- 2x^3 - 9x^2 - 12x + 1$ is strictly increasing or decreasing.

3. Find the intervals in which the function f(x) = $(x + 1)^3 (x - 3)^3$ is strictly increasing or decreasing.

4. Find the intervals in which the function f(x) = sinx + cosx , $0 \le x \le 2\pi$ is strictly increasing or decreasing.

5. Find the intervals in which the function f(x) = sin 3x, x $\in \left[0, \dfrac{\pi}{2}\right]$ is strictly increasing or decreasing.

6. Find the intervals in which the function f(x) = $\dfrac{4\sin x - 2x - x\cos x}{2 + \cos x}$ is strictly increasing or decreasing.

7. Find the intervals in which the function f(x) = $x^3 + \dfrac{1}{x^3}$, x $\ne 0$ is strictly increasing or decreasing.

8. Find the intervals in which the function $f(x) = x^4 - \dfrac{4x^3}{3}$ is strictly increasing or decreasing.

9. Show that y = $\log(1 + x) - \dfrac{2x}{2 + x}$, x >-1, is an increasing function of x throughout its domain.

10. Prove that $y = \dfrac{4\sin\theta}{(2 + \cos\theta)} - \theta$ is an increasing function in $\left[0, \dfrac{\pi}{2}\right]$.

11. Show that the function f(x) = $4x^3 - 18x^2 + 27x - 7$ is always increasing in R.

12. Find the intervals in which: $f(x) = \sin 3x - \cos 3x$, $0 < x < \pi$, is strictly increasing or strictly decreasing.

ANSWERS

1. ↑ in $(-\infty, -2) \cup (3, \infty)$ and ↓ in $(-2, 3)$

2. ↑ in $(-2, -1)$ and ↓ in $(-\infty, -2) \cup (-1, \infty)$

3. ↑ in $(1, 3) \cup (3, \infty)$ and ↓ in $(-\infty, -1) \cup (-1, 1)$

4. ↑ in $\left[0, \dfrac{\pi}{4}\right) \cup \left(\dfrac{5\pi}{4}, 2\pi\right]$ and ↓ in $\left(\dfrac{\pi}{4}, \dfrac{5\pi}{4}\right)$

5. ↑ in $\left[0, \dfrac{\pi}{6}\right]$ and ↓ in $\left[\dfrac{\pi}{6}, \dfrac{\pi}{2}\right]$

6. ↑ in $\left(0, \dfrac{\pi}{2}\right) \cup \left(\dfrac{3\pi}{2}, 2\pi\right)$ and ↓ in $\left(\dfrac{\pi}{2}, \dfrac{3\pi}{2}\right)$

7. ↑ in $(-\infty, -1) \cup (1, \infty)$ and ↓ in $(-1, 1)$

8. increasing in $[1, \infty)$ and decreasing in $(-\infty, 1]$

12. ↑ in $\left(0, \dfrac{\pi}{4}\right) \cup \left(\dfrac{7\pi}{12}, \dfrac{11\pi}{12}\right)$ and ↓ $\left(\dfrac{\pi}{4}, \dfrac{7\pi}{12}\right) \cup \left(\dfrac{11\pi}{12}, \pi\right)$.

MAXIMA & MINIMA
SHORT ANSWER TYPE QUESTIONS

1. Find the maximum and the minimum values, if any, of the function $f(x) = (3x - 1)^2 + 4$ on R.

2. Find the maximum and the minimum values, if any, of the function $f(x) = -(x - 3)^2 + 5$ on R

3. Find the maximum and the minimum values, if any, of the function $f(x) = |x + 2| + 3$ on R.

4. Find the maximum and the minimum values, if any, of the function $f(x) = 3 - |x + 1|$ on R.

5. Find the maximum and the minimum values, if any, of the function $f(x) = 9x^2 + 12x + 2$ on R.

6. Find the maximum and the minimum values, if any, of the function $f(x) = \sin 3x + 4$ on R.

7. Find the maximum and the minimum values, if any, of the function $f(x) = |\sin 4x + 3|$ on R.

8. Find the maximum and the minimum values, if any, of the function $f(x) = x^3 - 1$ on R.

9. Find the local maxima and local minima, if any, for the function $f(x) = x^2$. Find also the local maximum and the local minimum values, as the case may be.

10. Find the local maxima and local minima, if any, for the function $f(x) = (x - 4)^2$. Find also the local maximum and the local minimum values, as the case may be.

11. Find the local maxima and local minima, if any, for the function $f(x) = \sin 2x - x$, $-\pi/2 \le x \le \pi/2$. Find also the local maximum and the local minimum values, as the case may be.

12. Find the local maxima and local minima, if any, for the function $f(x) = \sin x - \cos x$, $0 < x < 2\pi$. Find also the local maximum and the local minimum values, as the case may be.

13. Find the local maxima and local minima, if any, for the function $f(x) = x^3 - 9x^2 + 15x + 11$. Find also the local maximum and the local minimum values, as the case may be.

14. Find the local maxima and local minima, if any, for the function $f(x) = x^4 - 62x^2 + 120x + 9$. Find also the local maximum and the local minimum values, as the case may be.

15. Find the absolute maximum and minimum values of the function f given by
$f(x) = x^3 - 12x^2 + 36x + 17$ in $[1, 10]$.

16. Find the absolute maximum and minimum values of the function f given by
$f(x) = \dfrac{1}{3}x^3 - 3x^2 + 5x + 8$ in $[0, 4]$.

17. Find the absolute maximum and minimum values of the function f given by
$f(x) = \sin x + \cos x$, $x \in [0, \pi]$.

18. Find the absolute maximum and minimum values of the function f given by

36

f(x) = 2cos2x – cos4x in [0 , π].

19. Find the absolute maximum and minimum values of the function f given by
f(x) = sin²x – cos x, x ∈ [0, π].

20. Find the absolute maximum and minimum values of the function f given by
f(x) = sinx(1 + cosx), x ∈ [0, π].

ANSWERS

Minimum Value = 5, no maximum

Maximum Value = – 2, no minimum

Maximum Value = – 2, Minimum Value = 5

Local max. value is 0 at x = 4 & local min. value is 0 at x = 0

1. Minimum Value = 4, no maximum   **2.** Maximum Value = 5, no minimum

3. Minimum Value = 3, no maximum   **4.** Maximum Value = 3, no minimum

5. Minimum Value = – 2, no maximum   **6.** Maximum Value = 3, Minimum Value = 5

7. Minimum = 2; Maximum = 4   **8.** Neither minimum nor maximum.

9. Local minimum value is 0 at x = 0   **10.** Local maximum value is 0 at x = 4

11. Local maximum value is $\frac{\sqrt{3}}{2} - \frac{\pi}{6}$ at $x = \frac{\pi}{6}$ & local minimum value is $\frac{\pi}{6} - \frac{\sqrt{3}}{2}$ – at $x = -\frac{\pi}{6}$

12. Local maximum value is $\sqrt{2}$ at $x = \frac{3\pi}{4}$ & local minimum value is $-\sqrt{2}$ at $x = -\frac{7\pi}{4}$

13. Local maximum value is 19 at x = 1 & local minimum value is 15 at x = 3.

14. Local maximum value is 68 at x = 1 & local minimum value is – 316 at x = 5.

15. Absolute maximum value = 177 at x =10, absolute minimum value = 17 at x = 6.

16. Absolute maximum value = $\frac{31}{3}$ at x =1, absolute minimum value = $\frac{4}{3}$ at x = 4.

17. Absolute maximum value = $\sqrt{2}$ at $x = \frac{\pi}{4}$, absolute minimum value = – 1 at x = π.

18. Absolute maximum value = $\frac{3}{2}$ at $x = \frac{\pi}{4}$, absolute minimum value = – 3 at $x = \frac{\pi}{2}$.

19. Absolute maximum value = $\frac{5}{4}$ at $x = \frac{2\pi}{3}$, absolute minimum value = – 1 at x = 0.

20. Absolute maximum value = $\frac{3\sqrt{3}}{4}$ at $x = \frac{\pi}{3}$, absolute minimum value = 0 at x = 0, π.

LONG ANSWER TYPE QUESTIONS

1. Find two numbers whose sum is 24 and whose product is as large as possible.

2. Show that the right circular cylinder of given surface and maximum volume is such that its height is equal to the diameter of the base.

3. Of all the closed cylindrical cans (right circular), of a given volume of 100 cubic centimetres, find the dimensions of the can which has the minimum surface area?

4. A square piece of tin of side 18 cm is to be made into a box without top, by cutting a square from each corner and folding up the flaps to form the box. What should be the side of the square to be cut off so that the volume of the box is the maximum possible.

5. A rectangular sheet of tin 45 cm by 24 cm is to be made into a box without top, by cutting off square from each corner and folding up the flaps. What should be the side of the square to be cut off so that the volume of the box is maximum ?

6. A wire of length 28 m is to be cut into two pieces. One of the pieces is to be made into a square and the other into a circle. What should be the length of the two pieces so that the combined area of the square and the circle is minimum?

7. Show that the right circular cone of least curved surface and given volume has an altitude equal to $\sqrt{2}$ time the radius of the base.

8. Show that the semi-vertical angle of the cone of the maximum volume and of given slant height is $\tan^{-1}\left(\sqrt{2}\right)$.

9. Show that semi-vertical angle of right circular cone of given surface area and maximum volume is $\sin^{-1}(1/3)$.

10. A tank with rectangular base and rectangular sides, open at the top is to be constructed so that its depth is 2 m and volume is 8 m^3. If building of tank costs Rs 70 per sqmetres for the base and ₹ 45 per square metre for sides. What is the cost of least expensive tank?

11. The sum of the perimeter of a circle and square is k, where k is some constant. Prove that the sum of their areas is least when the side of square is double the radius of the circle.

12. A window is in the form of a rectangle surmounted by a semicircular opening. The total perimeter of the window is 10 m. Find the dimensions of the window to admit maximum light through the whole opening.

13. Show that of all the rectangles inscribed in a given fixed circle, the square has the maximum area.

14. Prove that the volume of the largest cone that can be inscribed in a sphere of radius R is $\dfrac{8}{27}$ of the volume of the sphere.

15. Show that the altitude of the right circular cone of maximum volume that can be inscribed in a sphere of radius R is $\dfrac{4R}{3}$

16. Show that the height of the cylinder of maximum volume that can be inscribed in a sphere of radius R is $\dfrac{2R}{\sqrt{3}}$. Also find the maximum volume

17. Show that height of the cylinder of greatest volume which can be inscribed in a right circular cone of height h and semi vertical angle α is one-third that of the cone and the greatest volume of cylinder is $\dfrac{4}{27}\pi h^3 \tan^2\alpha$.

18. Find the maximum area of an isosceles triangle inscribed in the ellipse $\dfrac{x^2}{a^2}+\dfrac{y^2}{b^2}=1$ with its vertex at one end of the major axis.

19. A point on the hypotenuse of a triangle is at distance a and b from the sides of the triangle. Show that the maximum length of the hypotenuse is $\left(a^{2/3}+b^{2/3}\right)^{3/2}$.

20. If the sum of the hypotenuse and a side of a right angled triangle is given, show that the area of the triangle is maximum when the angle between them is $\pi/3$.

21. If the length of three sides of a trapezium other than the base is 10 cm each, find the area of the trapezium, when it is maximum.

22. A window has the shape of a rectangle surmounted by an equilateral triangle. If the perimeter of the window is 12 m, find the dimensions of the rectangle that will produce the largest area of the window.

23. Prove that the radius of the right circular cylinder of greatest curved surface area which can be inscribed in a given cone is half of that of the cone.

24. An open box with a square base is to be made out of a given quantity of cardboard of area c^2 square units. Show that the maximum volume of the box is $\dfrac{c^3}{6\sqrt{3}}$ cubic units.

ANSWERS

1. 12, 12

3. $r = \left(\dfrac{50}{\pi}\right)^{\frac{1}{3}}$, $h = \dfrac{100}{\pi}\left(\dfrac{\pi}{50}\right)^{\frac{2}{3}}$

4. 3 cm

5. 5 cm

6. $\dfrac{112}{\pi+4}$ cm, $\dfrac{28\pi}{\pi+4}$ cm

10. ₹1000

12. length $= 2x = \dfrac{20}{[\pi+4]}$ m and breadth $= \dfrac{10}{[\pi+4]}$ m

18. Area is max. when $\theta = \dfrac{2\pi}{3}$ and max area is $ab\left(1+\dfrac{1}{2}\right)\dfrac{\sqrt{3}}{2} = \dfrac{3\sqrt{3}}{4}$ ab.

21. $75\sqrt{3}$ cm^2

22. Length $= \dfrac{12}{6-\sqrt{3}}$ m and width $= \dfrac{18-6\sqrt{3}}{6-\sqrt{3}}$ m

INDEFINITE INTEGRALS
SOME IMPORTANT RESULTS/CONCEPTS

* $\int x^n dx = \dfrac{x^{n+1}}{n+1} + C$

* $\int 1.dx = x + C$

* $\int \dfrac{1}{x^n} dx = -\dfrac{1}{x^n} + C$

* $\int \dfrac{1}{\sqrt{x}} = 2\sqrt{x} + C$

* $\int \dfrac{1}{x} dx = \log_e x + C$

* $\int e^x dx = e^x + C$

* $\int a^x dx = \dfrac{a^x}{\log_e a} + C$

* $\int \sin x \, dx = -\cos x + C$

* $\int \cos x \, dx = \sin x + C$

* $\int \sec^2 x \, dx = \tan x + C$

* $\int \mathrm{cosec}^2 x \, dx = -\cot x + C$

* $\int \sec x.\tan x \, dx = \sec x + C$

* $\int \mathrm{cosec} x.\cot x \, dx = -\mathrm{cosec} x + C$

* $\int \tan x \, dx = -\log|\cos x| + C = \log|\sec x| + C$

* $\int \cot x \, dx = \log|\sin x| + C$

* $\int \sec x \, dx = \log|\sec x + \tan x| + C$

$\qquad = \log\left|\tan\left(\dfrac{x}{2} + \dfrac{\pi}{4}\right)\right| + C$

* $\int \mathrm{cosec} x \, dx = \log|\mathrm{cosec} x - \cot x| + C$

$\qquad = -\log|\mathrm{cosec} x + \cot x| + C$

$\qquad = \log\left|\tan\dfrac{x}{2}\right| + C$

* $\int \dfrac{dx}{x^2 - a^2} = \dfrac{1}{2a}\log\left|\dfrac{x-a}{x+a}\right| + C$, if $x > a$

* $\int \dfrac{dx}{a^2 - x^2} = \dfrac{1}{2a}\log\left|\dfrac{a+x}{a-x}\right| + C$, if $x > a$

* $\int \dfrac{dx}{x^2 + a^2} = \dfrac{1}{a}\tan^{-1}\dfrac{x}{a} + C, = -\dfrac{1}{a}\cot^{-1}\dfrac{x}{a} + C$

* $\int \dfrac{1}{\sqrt{a^2 - x^2}} dx = \sin^{-1}\dfrac{x}{a} + c = -\cos^{-1}\dfrac{x}{a} + C$

* $\int \dfrac{dx}{\sqrt{a^2 + x^2}} = \log|x + \sqrt{x^2 + a^2}| + C$

* $\int \dfrac{dx}{\sqrt{x^2 - a^2}} = \log|x + \sqrt{x^2 - a^2}| + C$

* $\int \sqrt{x^2 + a^2} \, dx = \dfrac{x}{2}\sqrt{x^2 + a^2} + \dfrac{a^2}{2}\log\left|x + \sqrt{x^2 + a^2}\right| + C$

* $\int \sqrt{x^2 - a^2} \, dx = \dfrac{x}{2}\sqrt{x^2 - a^2} - \dfrac{a^2}{2}\log\left|x + \sqrt{x^2 - a^2}\right| + C$

* $\int \sqrt{a^2 - x^2} \, dx = \dfrac{x}{2}\sqrt{a^2 - x^2} + \dfrac{a^2}{2}\sin^{-1}\dfrac{x}{a} + C$

* $\int \{f_1(x) \pm f_2(x) \pm ....f_n(x)\}dx$

$\qquad = \int f_1(x)dx \pm \int f_2(x)dx \pm .... \pm \int f_n(x)dx$

* $\int \lambda f(x)dx = \lambda \int f(x)dx + C$

* $\int u.v \, dx = u.\int v.dx - \int\left[\int v.dx\right]\dfrac{du}{dx}.dx$

SOME ILUSTRATIONS :

Q. Evaluate : $\int \dfrac{x+2}{\sqrt{x^2 + 5x + 6}}dx$

Sol. $\int \dfrac{x+2}{\sqrt{x^2 + 5x + 6}}dx = \dfrac{1}{2}\int \dfrac{2x + 5 - 5 + 4}{\sqrt{x^2 + 5x + 6}}dx \qquad \left[\because \dfrac{d}{dx}\left(x^2 + 5x + 6\right) = 2x + 5\right]$

$= \dfrac{1}{2}\int \dfrac{2x + 5}{\sqrt{x^2 + 5x + 6}}dx - \dfrac{1}{2}\int \dfrac{dx}{\sqrt{x^2 + 5x + 6}} \qquad \left[x^2 + 5x + 6 = t\right]$

$$= \frac{1}{2}\int \frac{dt}{\sqrt{t}} - \frac{1}{2}\int \frac{dx}{\sqrt{x^2 + 5x + \left(\frac{5}{2}\right)^2 - \frac{25}{4} + 6}}$$

$$= \frac{1}{2}.2\sqrt{t} + \int \frac{dx}{\sqrt{\left(x - \frac{5}{2}\right)^2 - \left(\frac{1}{2}\right)^2}}$$

$$= \sqrt{x^2 + 5x + 6} - \frac{1}{2}\log\left|x + \frac{5}{2} + \sqrt{x^2 + 5x + 6}\right| + C$$

Q. Evaluate : $\int \dfrac{x^2}{(x-1)(x-2)(x-3)}dx$

Sol. $I = \int \dfrac{x^2}{(x-1)(x-2)(x-3)}dx$

Let $\dfrac{x^2}{(x-1)(x-2)(x-3)} = \dfrac{A}{(x-1)} + \dfrac{B}{(x-2)} + \dfrac{C}{(x-3)}$

$\Rightarrow x^2 = A(x-2)(x-3) + B(x-1)(x-3) + C(x-2)(x-3)$

Putting $x = 1, 2, 3$ successively $\quad A = \dfrac{1}{2}, \quad B = -4, \quad C = \dfrac{9}{2}$

$I = \dfrac{1}{2}\int \dfrac{dx}{(x-1)} - 4\int \dfrac{dx}{(x-2)} + \dfrac{9}{2}\int \dfrac{dx}{(x-3)}$

$\quad = \dfrac{1}{2}\log|x-1| - 4\log|x-2| + \dfrac{9}{2}\log|x-3| + C$

Q. Evaluate : $\int \dfrac{x^2 + 2x + 8}{(x-1)(x-2)}dx$

Sol. $I = \int \dfrac{x^2 + 2x + 8}{(x-1)(x-2)}dx = \int \dfrac{x^2 + 2x + 8}{x^2 - 3x + 2}dx$

$\quad = \int \dfrac{x^2 - 3x + 2 + 5x + 6}{x^2 - 3x + 2}dx = \int \left(1 + \dfrac{5x+6}{x^2 - 3x + 2}\right)dx$

$\quad = \int 1.dx + \int \dfrac{5x+6}{(x-1)(x-2)}dx = x + I_1$

$I_1 = \int \dfrac{5x+6}{(x-1)(x-2)}dx$

Let $\dfrac{5x+6}{(x-1)(x-2)} = \dfrac{A}{(x-1)} + \dfrac{B}{(x-2)}$

$\Rightarrow 5x + 6 = A(x-2) + B(x-1)$

Putting $x = 1, 2 \Rightarrow A = -11, B = 16$

$\therefore I_1 = \int \dfrac{5x+6}{(x-1)(x-2)}dx = -11\log|x-1| + 16\log|x-2|$

$I = x - 11\log|x-1| + 16\log|x-2| + C$

Q.Evaluate : $\int x^2\tan^{-1}x.dx$

41

Sol. $\int x^2 \tan^{-1} x \, dx = \tan^{-1} x \int x^2 \, dx - \int \left[\left(\int x^2 \, dx \right) \frac{d}{dx} \left(\tan^{-1} x \right) \right] dx$

$= \tan^{-1} x . \dfrac{x^3}{3} - \int \dfrac{x^3}{3} . \dfrac{1}{1+x^2} \, dx = \tan^{-1} x . \dfrac{x^3}{3} - \dfrac{1}{3} \int \dfrac{x^3}{1+x^2} \, dx$

$= \tan^{-1} x . \dfrac{x^3}{3} - \dfrac{1}{3} \int \dfrac{x^3 + x - x}{1+x^2} \, dx$

$= \tan^{-1} x . \dfrac{x^3}{3} - \dfrac{1}{3} \int \dfrac{x(x^2 + 1) - x}{1+x^2} \, dx$

$= \tan^{-1} x . \dfrac{x^3}{3} - \dfrac{1}{3} \int x \, dx + \dfrac{1}{6} \int \dfrac{2x}{1+x^2} \, dx$

$= \dfrac{x^3}{3} \tan^{-1} x - \dfrac{1}{6} x^2 + \dfrac{1}{6} \log(x^2 + 1) + C$

Q. Evaluate : $\int \left(\sin^{-1} x \right)^2 dx$

Sol. $I = \int \left(\sin^{-1} x \right)^2 dx = \int 1 . \left(\sin^{-1} x \right)^2 dx$

$= \left(\sin^{-1} x \right)^2 \int 1 . dx - \int \left\{ \left(\int 1 . dx \right) \dfrac{d}{dx} \left(\sin^{-1} x \right)^2 \right\} dx$

$= \left(\sin^{-1} x \right)^2 . x - \int x . \dfrac{2 \left(\sin^{-1} x \right)}{\sqrt{1 - x^2}} \, dx = x(\sin^{-1} x)^2 - 2 \int \dfrac{x \sin^{-1} x}{\sqrt{1 - x^2}} \, dx$

$= x(\sin^{-1} x)^2 - 2 I_1 + C$

$I_1 = \int \dfrac{x \sin^{-1} x}{\sqrt{1 - x^2}} \, dx \qquad \text{Put} \quad \sin^{-1} x = t \Rightarrow \dfrac{1}{\sqrt{1 - x^2}} \, dx = dt$

$= \int t . \sin t . dt = t \int \sin t . dt + \int \cos t . dt = -t \cos t + \sin t$

$= -\sin^{-1} x . \sqrt{1 - x^2} + x$

$\therefore I = x(\sin^{-1} x)^2 - 2 \left[-\sin^{-1} x . \sqrt{1 - x^2} + x \right] + C$

SHORT ANSWER TYPE QUESTIONS

Evaluate the following integrals :

1. $\int e^{3 \log x} . x^4 dx$

2. $\int \dfrac{2 \cos x}{3 \sin^2 x} \, dx$

3. $\int a^{4 \log_a x} \, dx$

4. $\int \dfrac{e^{5;\text{og} x} - e^{4 \log x}}{e^{3 \log x} - e^{2 \log x}} \, dx$

5. $\int \cosec^2 (3 - 7x) \, dx$

6. $\int 3^{5 - 4x} \, dx$

7. $\int \sec^2 (4 - 5x) \, dx$

8. $\int \dfrac{x + 3}{x^2 + 4x + 3} \, dx$

9. $\int \dfrac{e^{\log \sqrt{x}}}{x} \, dx$

10. $\int \dfrac{1}{1 - \sin x} \, dx$

11. $\int \dfrac{1}{1 - \cos x} \, dx$

12. $\int \sqrt{1 + \sin x} \, dx$

13. $\int \sqrt{1-\cos 2x}\, dx$

14. $\int \sqrt{1-\sin 2x}\, dx,\ \dfrac{\pi}{4} < x < \dfrac{\pi}{2}$

15. $\int (1+x)\sqrt{x}\, dx$

16. $\int \dfrac{x}{\sqrt{x+3}}\, dx$

17. $\int \dfrac{1}{\sin^2 x \cos^2 x}\, dx$

18. $\int \dfrac{\sin^3 x + \cos^3 x}{\sin^2 x \cos^2 x}\, dx$

19. $\int \dfrac{1}{\sqrt{2x+3}+\sqrt{2x-3}}\, dx$

20. $\int \tan^{-1}\left[\sqrt{\dfrac{1-\sin x}{1+\sin x}}\right] dx$

21. $\int \dfrac{x^2+1}{(x+1)^2}\, dx$

22. $\int \dfrac{x}{\sqrt{x+3}}\, dx$

23. $\int \sin^2 x\, dx$

24. $\int \cos^2 x\, dx$

25. $\int \sin^3 x\, dx$

26. $\int \sin 4x \cos 3x\, dx$

27. $\int \cos 2x \cos 4x\, dx$

28. $\int \tan^2 x\, dx$

29. $\int \cot^2 x\, dx$

30. $\int 3^{x+2}\, dx$

ANSWERS

1. $x^8 + C$

2. $-\dfrac{2}{3}\operatorname{cosec} x + C$

3. $\dfrac{x^4}{x} + C$

4. $\dfrac{x^3}{3} + C$

5. $\dfrac{\cot(3-7x)}{7} + C$

6. $\dfrac{3^{5-4x}}{(-4)\log 3} + C$

7. $-\dfrac{\tan(4-5x)}{5} + C$

8. $\log|x| + C$

9. $2\sqrt{x} + C$

10. $\tan x + \sec x + C$

11. $-\cot x - \operatorname{cosec} x + C$

12. $2\left(\sin\dfrac{x}{2} - \cos\dfrac{x}{2}\right) + C$

13. $\sqrt{2}\sin x + C$

14. $-\cos x - \sin x + C$

15. $\dfrac{2}{3}x^{3/2} + \dfrac{2}{5}x^{5/2} + C$

16. $\dfrac{2}{3}\sqrt{x+3}(x-6) + C$

17. $-2\cot 2x + C$

18. $\sec x - \operatorname{cosec} x + C$

19. $\dfrac{1}{18}\left[(2x+3)^{3/2} - (2x-3)^{3/2}\right] + C$

20. $\dfrac{\pi}{4} - \dfrac{x}{2} + C$

21. $x - 2\log|x+1| - \dfrac{2}{x+1} + C$

22. $\dfrac{2}{3}\sqrt{x+3}(x-6) + C$

23. $\dfrac{1}{2}\left(x - \dfrac{\sin 2x}{2}\right) + C$

24. $\dfrac{1}{2}\left(x + \dfrac{\sin 2x}{2}\right) + C$

25. $\dfrac{1}{4}\left(-3\cos x + \dfrac{\cos 3x}{3}\right) + C$

26. $\dfrac{1}{2}\left(-\dfrac{\cos 7x}{7} - \cos x\right) + C$

27. $\dfrac{1}{2}\left(\dfrac{\sin 6x}{6}+\dfrac{\sin 2x}{2}\right)+C$

28. $\tan x - x + C$

29. $-\cot x - x - C$

30. $9\left(\dfrac{3^x}{\log 3}\right)+C$

LONG ANSWER TYPE QUESTIONS

Evaluate the following integrals :

1. $\displaystyle\int \dfrac{x+2}{\sqrt{x^2+5x+6}}dx$

2. $\displaystyle\int \dfrac{3x+5}{\sqrt{x^2-8x+7}}dx$

3. $\displaystyle\int \dfrac{(3x+1).dx}{\sqrt{5-2x-x^2}}$

4. $\displaystyle\int \dfrac{5x+3}{\sqrt{x^2+4x+10}}.dx$

5. $\displaystyle\int \dfrac{x+3}{\sqrt{5-4x-x^2}}.dx$

6. $\displaystyle\int \dfrac{6x+7}{\sqrt{(x-5)(x-4)}}dx$

7. $\displaystyle\int (x-3)\sqrt{x^2+4x+3}\ dx$

8. $\displaystyle\int (5x-1)\sqrt{6+5x-2x^2}\,dx$

9. $\displaystyle\int (x-4)\sqrt{4+3x-x^2}\ dx$

10. $\displaystyle\int \dfrac{x^2}{(x-1)(x-2)(x-3)}dx$

11. $\displaystyle\int \dfrac{3x-1}{(x-1)(x-2)(x-3)}dx$

12. $\displaystyle\int \dfrac{3x-2}{(x+1)^2(x+3)}dx$

13. $\displaystyle\int \dfrac{x^2+x+1}{(x+1)^2(x+2)}dx$

14. $\displaystyle\int \dfrac{1}{1+x^3}\,dx$

15. $\displaystyle\int \dfrac{x^2+x+1}{(x^2+1)(x+2)}dx$

16. $\displaystyle\int \dfrac{x^2+2x+8}{(x-1)(x-2)}dx$

17. $\displaystyle\int \dfrac{x^4}{(x-1)(x^2+1)}dx$

18. $\displaystyle\int \dfrac{dx}{\sin x + \sin 2x}$

19. $\displaystyle\int \dfrac{2\sin 2\varphi - \cos\varphi}{6-\cos^2\varphi - 4\sin\varphi}d\varphi$

20. $\displaystyle\int \sin^4 x\ dx$

21. $\displaystyle\int \cos^4 x.dx$

22. $\displaystyle\int \cos x.\cos 2x\cos 3x.dx$

23. $\displaystyle\int \sin^3 x.\cos^3 x.dx$

24. $\displaystyle\int \sin^5 x.dx$

25. $\displaystyle\int \dfrac{\sin^8 x - \cos^8 x}{1-2\sin^2 x.\cos^2 x}dx$

26. $\displaystyle\int \dfrac{dx}{a\sin^2 x + b\cos^2 x}$

27. $\displaystyle\int \dfrac{dx}{\cos x(\sin x + 2\cos x)}$

28. $\displaystyle\int \dfrac{dx}{5+4\sin x}$

29. $\displaystyle\int \dfrac{dx}{\sin x + \sqrt{3}\cos x}$

30. $\displaystyle\int \dfrac{dx}{\sin x - \sqrt{3}\cos x}$

31. $\displaystyle\int \dfrac{2\sin x + 3\cos x}{3\sin x + 4\cos x}dx$

32. $\displaystyle\int \dfrac{dx}{1-\tan x}$

33. $\displaystyle\int \dfrac{dx}{1+\cot x}$

34. $\displaystyle\int x^2\tan^{-1}x.dx$

44

35. $\int \left(\sin^{-1}x\right)^2 dx$

36. $\int \left(\log x\right)^2 dx$

37. $\int \sec^3 x \, dx$

38. $\int \dfrac{xe^x}{\left(x+1\right)^2} dx$

39. $\int \left(\dfrac{2+\sin 2x}{1+\cos 2x}\right) e^x dx$

40. $\int \left(\dfrac{1-\sin x}{1-\cos x}\right) e^x dx$

41. $\int \dfrac{x^2+1}{\left(x+1\right)^2} e^x dx$

42. $\int \left[\log(\log x) + \dfrac{1}{\left(\log x\right)^2}\right] dx$

43. $\int \dfrac{x-1}{\left(x+1\right)^3} e^x dx$

44. $\int \dfrac{2-x}{\left(1-x\right)^2} \cdot e^x dx$

45. $\int e^{2x}\sin 3x \, dx$

46. $\int e^x \sin^2 x \, dx$

47. $\int \dfrac{dx}{\sin(x-a)\cdot\sin(x-b)}$

48. $\int \dfrac{dx}{\cos(x-a)\cdot\cos(x-b)}$

49. $\int \dfrac{dx}{\cos(x+a)\cdot\cos(x+b)}$

50. $\int \dfrac{dx}{\sin(x+a)\cdot\cos(x+b)}$

51. $\int \dfrac{\cos(x+a)}{\sin(x+b)}\cdot dx$

52. $\int \dfrac{x^2+1}{x^4+1} dx$

53. $\int \dfrac{x^2+4}{x^4+16} dx$

54. $\int \dfrac{x^2-1}{x^4+x^2+1} dx$

55. $\int \dfrac{1}{x^4+x^2+1} dx$

56. $\int \sqrt{\tan x}\, dx$

57. $\int \dfrac{1}{\sin^4 x + \cos^4 x} dx$

58. $\int \dfrac{1}{x^4-5x^2+16} dx$

59. $\int \dfrac{dx}{\left(2x+3\right)\sqrt{4x+5}}$

60. $\int \dfrac{dx}{\left(x^2-4\right)\sqrt{x+1}}$

61. $\int \dfrac{dx}{\left(x+2\right)\sqrt{x^2+6x+5}}$

62. $\int \dfrac{dx}{\left(1+x^2\right)\sqrt{1-x^2}}$

ANSWERS

1. $\sqrt{x^2+5x+6} - \dfrac{1}{2}\log\left|x+\dfrac{5}{2}+\sqrt{x^2+5x+6}\right| + C$

2. $3\sqrt{x^2-8x+7} + 17\log\left|(x-4)+\sqrt{x^2-8x+7}\right| + C$

3. $-3\sqrt{5-2x-x^2} - 2\sin^{-1}\left(\dfrac{x+1}{\sqrt{6}}\right) + C$

4. $5\sqrt{x^2+4x+10} - 7\log\left|(x+2)+\sqrt{x^2+4x+10}\right| + C$

5. $-\sqrt{5-4x-x^2} + \sin^{-1}\left(\dfrac{x+2}{3}\right) + C$

6. $6\sqrt{x^2-9x+20} + 34\log\left|\left(x-\dfrac{9}{2}\right)+\sqrt{x^2-9x+20}\right| + C$

45

7. $\frac{1}{3}\left(x^2+4x+3\right)^{\frac{3}{2}}-5\left[\left(\frac{x+2}{2}\right)\sqrt{x^2+4x+3}-\frac{1}{2}\log\left|(x+2)+\sqrt{x^2+4x+3}\right|\right]+C$

8. $\frac{-5}{6}\left(6+5x-2x^2\right)^{\frac{3}{2}}+\frac{21\sqrt{2}}{4}\left[\left(\frac{4x-5}{8}\right)\sqrt{3+\frac{5}{2}x-x^2}+\frac{73}{32}\sin^{-1}\left(\frac{4x-5}{\sqrt{73}}\right)\right]+C$

9. $-\frac{1}{3}\left(4+3x-x^2\right)^{\frac{3}{2}}-\frac{5}{2}\left[\left(\frac{2x-3}{4}\right)\sqrt{4+3x-x^2}+\frac{25}{8}\sin^{-1}\left(\frac{2x-3}{5}\right)\right]+C$

10. $\frac{1}{2}\log|x-1|-4\log|x-2|+\frac{9}{2}\log|x-3|+C$

11. $\log|x-1|-5\log|x-2|+4\log|x-3|+C$

12. $\frac{11}{4}\log\left|\frac{x+1}{x+3}\right|+\frac{5}{2}\left(\frac{1}{x+1}\right)+C$

13. $-\log|x+1|-\frac{1}{x+1}+3\log|x+2|+C$

14. $\frac{1}{3}\log|1+x|-\frac{1}{6}\log\left|1-x+x^2\right|+\frac{1}{\sqrt{3}}\tan^{-1}\left(\frac{2x-1}{\sqrt{3}}\right)+C$

15. $\frac{3}{5}\log|x+2|+\frac{1}{5}\log\left(x^2+1\right)+\frac{1}{5}\tan^{-1}x+C$

16. $x-11\log|x-1|+16\log|x-2|+C$

17. $\frac{x^2}{2}+x+\frac{1}{2}\log|x-1|-\frac{1}{4}\log\left(x^2+1\right)-\frac{1}{2}\tan^{-1}x+C$

18. $\frac{1}{6}\log|\cos x-1|+\frac{1}{2}\log|\cos x+1|-\frac{2}{3}\log|1+2\cos x|+C$

19. $2\log\left|\sin^2\phi-4\sin\phi+5\right|+7\tan^{-1}(\sin\phi-2)+C$

20. $\frac{1}{4}\left[\frac{3}{2}x-\sin 2x+\frac{1}{8}\sin 4x\right]+C$

21. $\frac{1}{8}\left(3x+2\sin 2x+\frac{\sin 4x}{4}\right)+C$

22. $\frac{x}{4}+\frac{\sin 6x}{24}+\frac{\sin 4x}{16}+\frac{\sin 2x}{8}+C$

23. $\frac{\sin^4 x}{4}-\frac{\sin^6 x}{6}+C$

24. $-\cos x+\frac{2\cos^3 x}{3}-\frac{\cos^5 x}{5}+C$

25. $-\frac{\sin 2x}{2}+C$

26. $\frac{1}{\sqrt{ab}}\tan^{-1}\left(\frac{\sqrt{a}\tan x}{\sqrt{b}}\right)+C$

27. $\log|\tan x+2|+C$

28. $\frac{2}{3}\tan^{-1}\left(\frac{\tan x/2}{3}\right)+C$

29. $\frac{1}{2}\log\left|\frac{1+\sqrt{3}\tan x/2}{3-\sqrt{3}\tan x/2}\right|+C$

30. $\frac{1}{2}\log\left|\tan\left(\frac{x}{2}+\frac{\pi}{12}\right)\right|$

31. $\frac{18}{15}x+\frac{1}{25}\log|3\sin x+4\cos x|+C$

32. $\frac{x}{2}-\frac{1}{2}\log|\sin x-\cos x|$

33. $\frac{x}{2}-\frac{1}{2}\log|\sin x+\cos x|$

34. $\frac{x^3}{3}\tan^{-1}x-\frac{1}{6}x^2+\frac{1}{6}\log(x^2+1)+C$

35. $x(\sin^{-1}x)^2-2\left[-\sin^{-1}x.\sqrt{1-x^2}+x\right]+C$

36. $x(\log x)^2-2[x\log x-x]+C$

37. $\frac{1}{2}\sec x\tan x+\frac{1}{2}\log|\sec x+\tan x|+C$

38. $\frac{1}{x+1}e^x+C$

39. $e^x\tan x+C$

40. $-e^x\cot\frac{x}{2}+C$

41. $e^x-2\frac{e^x}{x+1}+C$

42. $x\log(\log x)-\frac{x}{\log x}+C$

43. $\frac{e^x}{(x+1)^2}+C$

44. $\frac{e^x}{1-x}+C$

45. $\frac{e^{2x}}{13}(2\sin 3x-3\cos 3x)+C$

46. $\frac{1}{2}e^x-\frac{e^x}{10}(\cos 2x+2\sin 2x)+C$

47. $\frac{1}{\sin(b-a)}\log\frac{\sin|x-b|}{\sin|x-a|}+C$

48. $\frac{1}{\sin(b-a)}\log\frac{\cos|x-b|}{\cos|x-a|}+C$

49. $\frac{1}{\sin(b-a)}\log\frac{\cos|x+a|}{\cos|x+b|}+C$

50. $\dfrac{1}{\cos(b-a)}\log\left|\dfrac{\sin(x+a)}{\cos(x+b)}\right|+C$

51. $\cos(a-b)\log\sin|x+b|-(x+b)\sin(b-a)+C$

52. $\dfrac{1}{\sqrt{2}}\tan^{-1}\left(\dfrac{x^2-1}{\sqrt{2}\,x}\right)+C$

53. $\dfrac{1}{2\sqrt{2}}\tan^{-1}\left(\dfrac{x^2-4}{2\sqrt{2}\,x}\right)+C$

54. $\dfrac{1}{2}\log\left|\dfrac{x^2-x+1}{x^2+x+1}\right|+C$

55. $\dfrac{1}{2\sqrt{3}}\tan^{-1}\left(\dfrac{x^2-1}{\sqrt{3}\,x}\right)-\dfrac{1}{4}\log\left|\dfrac{x^2-x+1}{x^2+x+1}\right|+C$

56. $\dfrac{1}{\sqrt{2}}\tan^{-1}\left(\dfrac{\tan x-1}{\sqrt{2}\,\tan x}\right)+\dfrac{1}{2\sqrt{2}}\log\left|\dfrac{\tan x-\sqrt{2}\tan x+1}{\tan x+\sqrt{2}\tan x+1}\right|+C$

57. $\dfrac{1}{\sqrt{2}}\tan^{-1}\left(\dfrac{\tan^2 x-1}{\sqrt{2}\,\tan x}\right)+C$

58. $\dfrac{1}{8\sqrt{3}}\tan^{-1}\left(\dfrac{x^2-4}{\sqrt{3}\,x}\right)-\dfrac{1}{16\sqrt{3}}\log\left|\dfrac{x^2-\sqrt{13}x+4}{x^2+\sqrt{13}x+4}\right|+C$

59. $\tan^{-1}\sqrt{4x+5}+C$

60. $\dfrac{1}{4\sqrt{3}}\log\left|\dfrac{\sqrt{x+1}-\sqrt{3}}{\sqrt{x+1}+\sqrt{3}}\right|-\dfrac{1}{2}\tan^{-1}\sqrt{x+1}+C$

61. $\sin^{-1}\left[-\dfrac{1}{\sqrt{2}}\left(\dfrac{x+1}{x+2}\right)\right]+C$

62. $-\dfrac{1}{\sqrt{2}}\tan^{-1}\sqrt{\dfrac{1-x^2}{2x^2}}+C$

DEFINITE INTEGRALS
SOME IMPORTANT RESULTS/CONCEPTS

* $\int_a^b f(x)\,dx = F(b) - F(a)$, where $F(x) = \int f(x)\,dx$

* $\int_a^b f(x)\,dx = \int_a^b f(t)\,dt$

* $\int_a^b f(x)\,dx = -\int_a^b f(x)\,dx$

* $\int_a^b f(x)\,dx = \int_a^c f(x)\,dx + \int_c^b f(x)\,dx$

* $\int_a^b f(x)\,dx = \int_a^b f(a+b-x)\,dx$

* $\int_0^a f(x)\,dx = \int_0^a f(a-x)\,dx$

* $\int_{-a}^a f(x)\,dx = \begin{cases} 2\int_0^a f(x)\,dx, & \text{if } f(x) \text{ is an even function of } x. \\ 0 & \text{if } f(x) \text{ is an odd function of } x \end{cases}$

* $\int_0^{2a} f(x)\,dx = \begin{cases} 2\int_0^a f(x)\,dx, & \text{if } f(2a-x) = f(x). \\ 0 & \text{if } f(2a-x) = -f(x) \end{cases}$

SOME ILUSTRATIONS :

Q. Evaluate $\int_0^{\pi} \dfrac{x\sin x}{1+\cos^2 x}\,dx$

Sol. $I = \int_0^{\pi} \dfrac{x\sin x}{1+\cos^2 x}\,dx$ ...(i)

Also $I = \int_0^{\pi} \dfrac{(\pi-x)\sin(\pi-x)}{1+\cos^2(\pi-x)}\,dx = \int_0^{\pi} \dfrac{(\pi-x)\sin x}{1+\cos^2 x}\,dx$ ...(ii)

$2I = \pi\int_0^{\pi} \dfrac{\sin x}{1+\cos^2 x}\,dx$ Put $\cos x = t \Rightarrow -\sin x\,dx = dt$

$x = 0 \Rightarrow t = 1, x = \pi \Rightarrow t = -1$

$\therefore 2I = -\pi\int_1^{-1} \dfrac{dt}{1+t^2} = -\pi\left[\tan^{-1} t\right]_1^{-1} = -\pi\left[\tan^{-1}(-1) - \tan^{-1} 1\right]$

$= -\pi\left[-\dfrac{\pi}{4} - \dfrac{\pi}{4}\right] = \dfrac{\pi^2}{2}$ $\therefore I = \dfrac{\pi^2}{4}.$

Q. Evaluate : $\int_0^{\pi/2} \dfrac{\sin^3 x}{\sin^3 x + \cos^3 x}\,dx$

49

Sol. $I = \int\limits_0^{\pi/2} \dfrac{\sin^3 x}{\sin^3 x + \cos^3 x} dx$ ...(i)

Also $I = \int\limits_0^{\pi/2} \dfrac{\cos^3 x}{\cos^3 x + \sin^3 x} dx$ ...(ii)

$\therefore 2I = \int\limits_0^{\pi/2} 1.dx = [x]_0^{\pi/2} = \dfrac{\pi}{2}$

$\therefore I = \dfrac{\pi}{4}$

Q. Evaluate : $\int\limits_0^{\pi} \dfrac{x\tan x}{\sec x + \tan x} dx$

Sol. $I = \int\limits_0^{\pi} \dfrac{x\tan x}{\sec x + \tan x} dx$

Also $I = \int\limits_0^{\pi} \dfrac{(\pi - x)\tan(\pi - x)}{\sec(\pi - x) + \tan(\pi - x)} dx = \int\limits_0^{\pi} \dfrac{(\pi - x)\tan x}{\sec x + \tan x} dx$

$\therefore 2I = \pi\int\limits_0^{\pi} \dfrac{\tan x}{\sec x + \tan x} dx = \pi\int\limits_0^{\pi} \dfrac{\tan x}{\sec x + \tan x} \times \dfrac{\sec x - \tan x}{\sec x - \tan x} dx$

$= \pi\int\limits_0^{\pi} \dfrac{\tan x.\sec x - \tan^2 x}{\sec^2 x - \tan^2 x} dx = \pi\int\limits_0^{\pi} \left(\tan x.\sec x - \tan^2 x\right) dx$

$= \pi\int\limits_0^{\pi} \left(\tan x.\sec x - \sec^2 x + 1\right) dx = \pi\left[\sec x - \tan x + x\right]_0^{\pi}$

$= \pi\left[\{\sec\pi - \tan\pi + \pi\} - \{\sec 0 - \tan 0 + 0\}\right] = \pi\left[-1 + \pi - 1\right]$

$= \pi\left[\pi - 2\right]$

$\therefore I = \dfrac{\pi}{2}\left[\pi - 2\right]$

Q. Evaluate: $\int\limits_1^{4} \left[|x - 1| + |x - 2| + |x - 4|\right] dx$.

Sol. $\int\limits_1^{4} \left[|x - 1| + |x - 2| + |x - 4|\right] dx$

$= \int\limits_1^{4} (x - 1)dx + \int\limits_1^{2} -(x - 2)dx + \int\limits_2^{4} (x - 2)dx + \int\limits_1^{4} -(x - 4)dx$

$= \dfrac{1}{2}\left[(x - 1)^2\right]_1^{4} - \dfrac{1}{2}\left[(x - 2)^2\right]_1^{2} + \dfrac{1}{2}\left[(x - 2)^2\right]_2^{4} - \dfrac{1}{2}\left[(x - 4)^2\right]_1^{4}$

$= \dfrac{1}{2}[9 - 0] - \dfrac{1}{2}[0 - 1] + \dfrac{1}{2}[4 - 0] - \dfrac{1}{2}[0 - 9]$

$= \dfrac{9}{2} + \dfrac{1}{2} + \dfrac{4}{2} + \dfrac{9}{2} = \dfrac{23}{2}$

SHORT ANSWER TYPE QUESTIONS

Evaluate the following integrals :

1. $\displaystyle\int_{-\pi/2}^{\pi/2} \frac{\cos x}{1+e^x} dx$

2. $\displaystyle\int_{-\pi/2}^{\pi/2} \sin^5 x \, dx$

3. $\displaystyle\int_{0}^{\pi} \cos^5 x \, dx$

4. $\displaystyle\int_{-\pi/2}^{\pi/2} x\cos^4 x \, dx$

5. $\displaystyle\int_{-\pi/2}^{\pi/2} \left(x\sin^4 x + \tan^5 x + 1\right) dx$

6. $\displaystyle\int_{-\pi/2}^{\pi/2} |\sin x| \, dx$

7. $\displaystyle\int_{0}^{\pi} |\cos x| \, dx$

8. $\displaystyle\int_{-1}^{1} e^{|x|} \, dx$

9. $\displaystyle\int_{-\pi/2}^{\pi/2} \sin^2 x \, dx$

10. $\displaystyle\int_{-1}^{1} x|x| \, dx$

11. $\displaystyle\int_{0}^{\pi/2} \frac{\sin^3 x}{\sin^3 x + \cos^3 x} dx$

12. $\displaystyle\int_{0}^{\pi/2} \frac{\sin^n x \, . dx}{\sin^n x + \cos^n x}$

13. $\displaystyle\int_{0}^{\pi/2} \frac{\cos^n x \, . dx}{\sin^n x + \cos^n x}$

14. $\displaystyle\int_{0}^{\pi/2} \frac{dx}{1 + \tan^n x}$

15. $\displaystyle\int_{0}^{\pi/2} \frac{dx}{1 + \cot^n x}$

16. $\displaystyle\int_{\pi/6}^{\pi/3} \frac{1}{1 + \sqrt{\tan x}} dx$

17. $\displaystyle\int_{\pi/6}^{\pi/3} \frac{1}{1 + \tan^n x} dx$

18. $\displaystyle\int_{\pi/6}^{\pi/3} \frac{dx}{1 + \cot^n x}$

19. $\displaystyle\int_{\pi/6}^{\pi/3} \frac{\sin^n x \, . dx}{\sin^n x + \cos^n x}$

20. $\displaystyle\int_{\pi/6}^{\pi/3} \frac{\cos^n x \, . dx}{\sin^n x + \cos^n x} dx$

21. $\displaystyle\int_{3}^{4} \frac{\sqrt{7-x}}{\sqrt{x} + \sqrt{7-x}} dx$

Answer

1. 1

2. 0

3. 0

4. 0

5. 0

6. 2

7. 2

8. $2e - 2$

9. $\dfrac{\pi}{2}$

10. 0

11. $\dfrac{\pi}{4}$

12. $\dfrac{\pi}{4}$

13. $\dfrac{\pi}{4}$

14. $\dfrac{\pi}{4}$

15. $\dfrac{\pi}{4}$

16. $\dfrac{\pi}{12}$

17. $\dfrac{\pi}{12}$

18. $\dfrac{\pi}{12}$

19. $\dfrac{\pi}{12}$

20. $\dfrac{\pi}{12}$

21. $\dfrac{1}{2}$

LONG ANSWER TYPE QUESTIONS

Evaluate the following integrals :

1. $\int_0^\pi \dfrac{x\tan x}{\sec x.\csc x}dx$

2. $\int_0^{\pi/4} \log(1+\tan x)dx$

3. $\int_0^{\pi/2} \dfrac{\sin^2 x}{\sin x + \cos x}$

4. $\int_0^{\pi/2} \dfrac{x}{\sin x + \cos x}$

5. $\int_0^\pi \dfrac{x\sin x}{1+\cos^2 x}dx$

6. $\int_0^{\pi/2} \dfrac{\sin 2x}{\sin^4 x + \cos^4 x}$

7. $\int_0^{\pi/2} \dfrac{x\sin x.\cos x}{\sin^4 x + \cos^4 x}dx$

8. $\int_{\pi/4}^{\pi/2} \cos 2x.\log\sin x\, dx$

9. $\int_0^\pi \dfrac{x}{1+\sin x}dx$

10. $\int_0^{\pi/4} \sqrt{1-\sin 2x}\, dx$

11. $\int_0^1 \sqrt{\dfrac{1-x}{1+x}}\, dx$

12. $\int_0^{\pi/2} \left(\sqrt{\tan x} + \sqrt{\cot x}\right)dx$

13. $\int_{\pi/6}^{\pi/3} \dfrac{\sin x + \cos x}{\sqrt{\sin 2x}}dx$

14. $\int_0^\pi \dfrac{dx}{5+4\cos x}$

15. $\int_0^1 |5x-3|dx$

16. $\int_1^4 \left[|x-1|+|x-2|+|x-4|\right]dx$

17. $\int_0^2 \left|x^2+2x-3\right|dx$

18. $\int_{-1}^2 \left|x^3 - x\right|dx$

19. $\int_{-1}^{3/2} |x\sin \pi x|dx$

20. $\int_0^{3/2} |x\cos \pi x|dx$

21. $\int_{-\pi/2}^{\pi/2} \left[\sin|x| - \cos|x|\right]dx$

22. $\int_0^\pi \dfrac{x\tan x}{\sec x + \tan x}dx$

23. $\int_0^{\pi/2} \log\sin x\, dx$ OR $\int_0^{\pi/2} \log\cos x\, dx$

24. $\int_0^1 2\tan^{-1} x^2\, dx$

25. $\int_0^a \sin^{-1}\sqrt{\dfrac{x}{a+x}}\, dx$

26. $\int_0^\pi \dfrac{x}{a^2\cos^2 x + b^2\sin^2 x}dx$

27. $\int_1^2 \dfrac{5x^2}{x^2+4x+3}dx$

28. $\int_0^{\pi/2} 2\sin x.\cos x.\tan^{-1}(\sin x)dx$

29. $\int_0^{\pi/2} \dfrac{x+\sin x}{1+\cos x}dx$

30. $\int_0^{\pi/4} \dfrac{\sin x + \cos x}{9+16\sin 2x}dx$

31. $\displaystyle\int_0^{\pi/2} \frac{\cos^2 x}{\cos^2 x + 4\sin^2 x}\, dx$

32. $\displaystyle\int_0^{\pi/2} (2\log\sin x - \log\sin 2x)\, dx$

OR $\displaystyle\int_0^{\pi/2} (2\log\cos x - \log\sin 2x)\, dx$

33. $\displaystyle\int_{\pi/2}^{\pi} \left[\frac{1-\sin x}{1-\cos x}\right] e^x\, dx$

34. $\displaystyle\int_0^1 \frac{\log(1+x)}{1+x^2}\, dx$

35. $\displaystyle\int_0^1 \log\left(\frac{1}{x} - 1\right) dx$

36. $\displaystyle\int_0^{\pi} \frac{e^{\cos x}}{e^{\cos x} + e^{-\cos x}}\, dx$

37. $\displaystyle\int_0^{2\pi} \frac{1}{1 + e^{\sin x}}\, dx$

38. $\displaystyle\int_0^1 x^2 (1-x)^n\, dx$

39. $\displaystyle\int_0^1 x \left(\tan^{-1} x\right)^2 dx$

40. $\displaystyle\int_0^{\pi} \log(1 + \cos x)\, dx$

41. $\displaystyle\int_0^1 \cot^{-1}\left(1 - x + x^2\right) dx$

ANSWERS

1. $\dfrac{\pi^2}{4}$

2. $\dfrac{\pi}{8}\log 2$

3. $\dfrac{1}{\sqrt{2}}\log\left(\sqrt{2} + 1\right)$

4. $\dfrac{\pi}{2\sqrt{2}}\log\left(\sqrt{2} + 1\right)$

5. $\dfrac{\pi^2}{4}$

6. $\dfrac{\pi}{2}$

7. $\dfrac{\pi^2}{16}$

8. $\dfrac{1}{4}\log 2 - \dfrac{\pi}{8} + \dfrac{1}{4}$

9. π

10. $\sqrt{2} - 1$

11. $\dfrac{\pi}{2} - 1$

12. $\sqrt{2}\,\pi$

13. $2\sin^{-1}\left(\dfrac{\sqrt{3}-1}{2}\right)$

14. $\dfrac{\pi}{3}$

15. $\dfrac{13}{10}$

16. $\dfrac{23}{2}$

17. 4

18. $\dfrac{11}{4}$

19. $\dfrac{3}{\pi} + \dfrac{1}{\pi^2}$

20. $\dfrac{5}{2\pi} - \dfrac{1}{\pi^2}$

21. 0

22. $\dfrac{\pi}{2}[\pi - 2]$

23. $\dfrac{\pi}{2}\log 2$

24. $\dfrac{\pi}{2} - \dfrac{\pi}{2\sqrt{2}} + \dfrac{1}{2\sqrt{2}}\log\dfrac{2-\sqrt{2}}{2+\sqrt{2}}$

25. $a\left(\dfrac{\pi-2}{2}\right)$

26. $\dfrac{\pi^2}{2ab}$

27. $5+10\log\dfrac{8}{15}+\dfrac{25}{2}\log\dfrac{6}{5}$

28. $\dfrac{\pi}{2}-1$

29. $\dfrac{\pi}{2}$

30. $\dfrac{1}{40}\log 9$

31. $\dfrac{\pi}{6}$

32. $\dfrac{\pi}{2}\log\dfrac{1}{2}$

33. $e^{\frac{\pi}{2}}$

34. $\dfrac{\pi}{8}\log 2$

35. 0

36. $\dfrac{\pi}{2}$

37. π

38. $\dfrac{2}{(n+1)(n+2)(n+3)}$

39. $\dfrac{\pi^2}{16}-\dfrac{\pi}{4}+\dfrac{1}{2}\log 2$

40. $-\pi\log 2$

41. $\dfrac{\pi}{2}-\log 2$

APPLICATIONS OF THE INTEGRALS
SOME IMPORTANT RESULTS/CONCEPTS

** Area of the region PQRSP $= \int\limits_{a}^{b} dA = \int\limits_{a}^{b} y\ dx = \int\limits_{a}^{b} f(x)\ dx$.

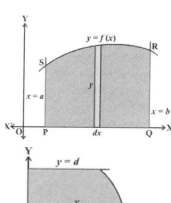

** The area A of the region bounded by the curve x = g (y), y-axis and

the lines y = c, y = d is given by $A = \int\limits_{c}^{d} x\ dy = \int\limits_{c}^{d} g(y)\ dy$

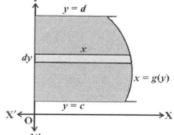

LONG ANSWER TYPE QUESTIONS
QUESTIONS FROM NCERT BOOK

1. Find the area enclosed by the circle $x^2 + y^2 = a^2$.

2. Find the area enclosed by the ellipse $\dfrac{x^2}{a^2} + \dfrac{y^2}{b^2} = 1$.

3. Find the area of the region bounded by the curve $y^2 = x$ and the lines x = 1, x = 4 and the x-axis.
4. Find the area of the region bounded by $y^2 = 9x$, x = 2, x = 4 and the x-axis in the first quadrant.

5. Find the area of the region bounded by the ellipse $\dfrac{x^2}{16} + \dfrac{y^2}{9} = 1$.

6. Find the area of the region bounded by the ellipse $\dfrac{x^2}{4} + \dfrac{y^2}{9} = 1$.

7. Find the area lying in the first quadrant and bounded by the circle $x^2 + y^2 = 4$ and the lines x = 0 and x = 2

8. Find the area of the region bounded by the curve $y^2 = 4x$, y-axis and the line y = 3

9. Find the area of the region bounded by the line y = 3x + 2, the x-axis and the ordinates x = –1 and x = 1.

10. Find the area under the given curves and given lines: $y = x^2$, x = 1, x = 2 and x-axis.

11. Find the area under the given curves and given lines: $y = x^4$, x = 1, x = 5 and x-axis.

12. Sketch the graph of y = |x + 3| and evaluate $\int\limits_{-6}^{0} |x + 3| dx$.

13. Find the area bounded by the curve y = sin x between x = 0 and x = 2π.

14. Find the area bounded by the curve $y = x^3$, the x-axis and the ordinates x = – 2 and x = 1.

15. Find the area bounded by the curve y = x | x | , x-axis and the ordinates x = – 1 and x = 1.

ANSWERS

1. πa^2 sq units.

2. πab sq units.

3. $\dfrac{14}{3}$ sq units.

4. $16 - 4\sqrt{2}$ sq units.

5. 12π sq units.

6. 6π sq units.

7. π sq units.

8. $\dfrac{9}{4}$ sq units.

9. $\dfrac{13}{3}$ sq units.

10. $\dfrac{7}{3}$ sq units.

11. 624.8 sq units.

12. 9 sq units.

13. 4 sq units.

14. $\dfrac{17}{4}$ sq units.

15. $\dfrac{2}{3}$ sq units.

DIFFERENTIAL EQUATIONS
SOME IMPORTANT RESULTS/CONCEPTS

** Order of Differential Equation : Order of the heighest order derivative of the given differential equation is called the order of the differential equation.

** Degree of the Differential Equation : Heighest power of the heighest order derivative when powers of all the derivatives are of the given differential equation is called the degree of the differential equatin

** Homogeneous Differential Equation : $\dfrac{dy}{dx} = \dfrac{f_1(x, y)}{f_2(x, y)}$, where $f_1(x, y) \& f_2(x, y)$ be the homogeneous function of same degree.

** Linear Differential Equation :

i. $\dfrac{dy}{dx} + py = q$, where $p \& q$ be the function of x or constant.

Solution of the equation is : $y.e^{\int p\,dx} = \int e^{\int p\,dx}.q\,dx$, where $e^{\int p\,dx}$ is Integrating Factor (I.F.)

ii. $\dfrac{dx}{dy} + px = q$, where $p \& q$ be the function of y or constant.

Solution of the equation is: $x.e^{\int p\,dy} = \int e^{\int p\,dy}.q\,dy$, where $e^{\int p\,dy}$ is Integrating Factor (I.F.)

SOME ILUSTRATIONS :

Q. Solve$(3xy - y^2)dx + (x^2 + xy)dy = 0$.

Sol. $\dfrac{dy}{dx} = \dfrac{y^2 - 3xy}{x^2 + xy}$ is a homogeneous differential equation

Put $y = vx \Rightarrow \dfrac{dy}{dx} = v + x\dfrac{dv}{dx}$

$\therefore v + x\dfrac{dv}{dx} = \dfrac{v^2 - 3xvx}{x^2 + xvx} = \dfrac{v^2x^2 - 3xvx}{x^2 + xvx} = \dfrac{v^2 - 3v}{1 + v}$

$\therefore x\dfrac{dv}{dx} = \dfrac{v^2 - 3v}{1 + v} - v = \dfrac{v^2 - 3v - v - v^2}{1 + v} = \dfrac{-4v}{1 + v}$

$\therefore \int\left(\dfrac{1 + v}{v}\right)dv = -4\int\dfrac{dx}{x} \Rightarrow \int\left(\dfrac{1}{v}\right)dv + \int dv = -4\int\dfrac{dx}{x}$

$\Rightarrow \log v + v + 4\log x = C \Rightarrow \log\dfrac{y}{x}.x^4 + \dfrac{y}{x} = C$

$\Rightarrow \mathbf{x\log(x^3 y) = Cx}$

Q. Show that following differential equation is homogeneous, and then solve it :

$2ye^{x/y}dx + \left(y - 2xe^{x/y}\right)dy = 0$, given that $y = 1$, when $x = 0$.

Sol. $2ye^{x/y}dx + \left(y - 2xe^{x/y}\right)dy = 0 \Rightarrow \dfrac{dx}{dy} = \dfrac{2xe^{x/y} - y}{2y.e^{x/y}}$

Let $F(x, y) = \dfrac{2xe^{x/y} - y}{2y.e^{x/y}}$

$F(\lambda x, \lambda y) = \dfrac{2\lambda xe^{\lambda x/\lambda y} - \lambda y}{2\lambda y.e^{\lambda x/\lambda y}} = \lambda^0\left(\dfrac{2xe^{x/y} - y}{2y.e^{x/y}}\right) = \lambda^0 F(x, y)$

57

$\therefore$ given Diff. Eq. is homogeneous. Put $x = vy \Rightarrow \dfrac{dx}{dy} = v + x\dfrac{dv}{dy}$

$\Rightarrow v + x\dfrac{dv}{dy} = \dfrac{2vye^{vy/y} - y}{2y.e^{vy/y}} = \dfrac{2ve^{v} - 1}{2.e^{v}}$

$\Rightarrow x\dfrac{dv}{dy} = \dfrac{2ve^{v} - 1}{2.e^{v}} - v = \dfrac{2ve^{v} - 1 - 2ve^{v}}{2.e^{v}} = -\dfrac{1}{2.e^{v}}$

$2\int e^{v}dv = -\int\dfrac{dy}{y} \Rightarrow 2e^{v} + \log|y| = C \Rightarrow 2e^{x/y} + \log|y| = C$

$\because y = 1$ when $x = 0 \Rightarrow C = 2$

$\therefore$ required sol. is $\mathbf{2e^{x/y} + \log|y| = C}$

Q. Solve : $\mathbf{x\log x\dfrac{dy}{dx} + y = 2\log x}$

Sol. $x\log x\dfrac{dy}{dx} + y = 2\log x \Rightarrow \dfrac{dy}{dx} + \dfrac{y}{x\log x} = \dfrac{2}{x}$ is a linear differential equation.

$P = \dfrac{1}{x\log x}, Q = \dfrac{2}{x}, \quad \text{I.F.} = e^{\int\frac{1}{x\log x}dx} = e^{\log(\log x)} = \log x$

Sol. is $y.\log x = \int\dfrac{2}{x}\log x\, dx + C = 2.\dfrac{(\log x)^{2}}{2} + C$

$\Rightarrow \mathbf{y\log x = (\log x)^{2} + C}$

Q. Solve : $\dfrac{\mathbf{dy}}{\mathbf{dx}} + \mathbf{2y\tan x = \sin x}; \mathbf{y\left(\dfrac{\pi}{3}\right) = 0}$

Sol. $\dfrac{dy}{dx} + 2y\tan x = \sin x$

$P = 2\tan x, Q = \sin x, \text{ I.F.} = e^{\int 2\tan x\, dx} = e^{2\log\sec x} = \sec^{2}x$

Sol. is. $y.\sec^{2}x = \int\sin x.\sec^{2}x\, dx + C = \int\sec x.\tan x\, dx + C$

$\Rightarrow y.\sec^{2}x = \sec x + C, \qquad y = 0, x = \dfrac{\pi}{3} \Rightarrow C = -2$

$\Rightarrow y.\sec^{2}x = \sec x - 2 \Rightarrow \mathbf{y = \cos x - 2\cos^{2}x}$

SHORT ANSWER TYPE QUESTIONS

1. Write the order and degree, if defined, of the differential equation :

$\left(\dfrac{d^{2}y}{dx^{2}}\right)^{3} - 4\left(\dfrac{dy}{dx}\right)^{4} + \sin(e^{x}) + y = 0.$

2. Write the order and degree, if defined, of the differential equation : $\left(\dfrac{d^{3}y}{dx^{3}}\right)^{2} - \sin x\left(\dfrac{dy}{dx}\right)^{4} + \cos y = 0.$

3. Write the order and degree, if defined, of the differential equation :

$$\left(\frac{d^2y}{dx^2}\right)^2 - \sin\left(\frac{dy}{dx}\right) + \sin(e^x) + y = 0.$$

4. Write the order and degree, if defined, of the differential equation : $\left(\frac{d^2y}{dx^2}\right)^2 - e^{\frac{dy}{dx}} + y = 0.$

5. Write the order and degree, if defined, of the differential equation : $\left(\frac{d^2y}{dx^2}\right)^{\frac{3}{2}} = \left(\frac{dy}{dx}\right)^2 + 1$

6. Write the order and degree, if defined, of the differential equation : $\left(\frac{d^2y}{dx^2}\right)^{\frac{2}{3}} = \left(y + \frac{dy}{dx}\right)^{\frac{1}{2}}$

7. Write the order and degree, if defined, of the differential equation : $\left[4 + \left(\frac{dy}{dx}\right)^2\right]^{7/3} = \frac{d^3y}{dx^3}$

8. If p and q are the degree and order of the differential equation $x\left(\frac{d^2y}{dx^2}\right)^3 + y\left(\frac{dy}{dx}\right)^4 + x^3 = 0$

respectively, then find the value of $2p - q$.

9. Solve : $dy + \sin x \sin y\, dx = 0$

10. Solve : $\dfrac{dy}{dx} = \dfrac{y}{x}$

11. Solve : $(1 + x^2)\dfrac{dy}{dx} = 1$

12. Solve : $\dfrac{dy}{dx} = e^{x+y}$

13. Solve : $\sec^2 x \tan y\, dx + \sec^2 y \tan x\, dy$

14. Solve : $\dfrac{dy}{dx} = 1 + x + y + xy$

15. Solve : $\dfrac{dy}{dx} = e^{x-y} + x^2 e^{-y}$

16. Solve : $(e^x + e^{-x})\dfrac{dy}{dx} = (e^x - e^{-x})$

17. Solve : $y \log y\, dx - x\, dy = 0$

18. Solve : $\cos x(1 + \cos y)dx - \sin y(1 + \sin x)dy = 0$

19. Solve : $3e^x \tan y\, dx + (1 - e^x)\sec^2 y\, dy = 0$

20. Solve : $(x + 2)\dfrac{dy}{dx} = 4x^2 y$

21. Solve : $x\sqrt{1 + y^2}\, dx + y\sqrt{1 + x^2}\, dy = 0$

22. Solve : $\dfrac{dy}{dx} = 1 + x + y + xy, \quad y(1) = 0$

23. Solve : $(1 + e^{2x})dy + (1 + y^2)e^x dx = 0, \quad y(0) = 1$

1. Order : 2 , Degree : 3

2. Order : 3 , Degree : 2

3. Order : 2 , Degree : Not defined

4. Order : 2 , Degree : Not defined

5. Order : 2 , Degree : 3

6. Order : 2 , Degree : 4

7. Order : 3 , Degree : 3

8. 4

9. $e^{-\cos x}\tan\dfrac{y}{2} = c$

10. $y = kx$

11. $y = \tan^{-1}x + c$

12. $-e^{-y} = e^x + C$

13. $\tan x.\tan y = C$

14. $\log(1 + y) = x + \dfrac{x^2}{2} + c$

15. $e^y = e^x + \dfrac{x^3}{3} + c$

16. $y = \log\left|e^x + e^{-x}\right| + C$

17. $y = e^{kx}$

18. $(1 + \sin x)(1 + \cos y) = C$

19. $(e^x - 1)^3 = C\tan y$

20. $\log y = 4\left\{\dfrac{x^2}{2} - 2x + 4\log(x + 2)\right\} + C$

21. $\sqrt{1 + x^2} + \sqrt{1 + y^2} = C$

22. $\log|1 + y| = x + \dfrac{x^2}{2} - \dfrac{3}{2}$

23. Ans. $\tan^{-1}y + \tan^{-1}\left(e^x\right) = \dfrac{\pi}{2}$

LONG ANSWER TYPE QUESTIONS
HOMOGENEOUS DIFFERENTIAL EQUATIONS

Show that following differential equation is homogeneous and hence solve it

1. Solve $(x^2 - y^2)dx + 2xydy = 0$, given that $y = 1$, when $x = 1$.

2. Solve $\dfrac{dy}{dx} = \dfrac{x(2y - x)}{x(2y + x)}$, given that $y = 1$, when $x = 1$.

3. Solve $(3xy - y^2)dx + (x^2 + xy)dy = 0$.

4. Solve $\dfrac{dy}{dx} - \dfrac{y}{x} + \csc\left(\dfrac{y}{x}\right)$, given that $y = 0$, when $x = 1$.

5. Solve $x\dfrac{dy}{dx} = y - x\tan\left(\dfrac{y}{x}\right)$.

6. Solve $(x^3 + y^3)dy - x^2ydx = 0$

7. Solve $x^2dy + (xy + y^2)dx = 0$, given that $y = 1$, when $x = 1$.

8. Show that following differential equation is homogeneous and hence solve it $(x - y)\dfrac{dy}{dx} = x + 2y$

9. Show that following diff. eq. is homogeneous, and then solve it $ydx + x\log\left(\dfrac{y}{x}\right) - 2xdy = 0$

10. Solve $xdy - ydx = \sqrt{x^2 + y^2}\,dx$

11. Solve $2x^2 \dfrac{dy}{dx} - 2xy + y^2 = 0$

12. Solve $x\dfrac{dy}{dx} - y + \sin\left(\dfrac{y}{x}\right) = 0$, given that $y = \pi$, when $x = 2$.

13. Show that following diff. eq. is homogeneous, and then solve it

$2ye^{x/y}dx + \left(y - 2xe^{x/y}\right)dy = 0$, given that $y = 1$, when $x = 0$.

14. Show that following diff. eq. is homogeneous, and then solve it

$x\dfrac{dy}{dx}.\sin\left(\dfrac{y}{x}\right) + x - y\sin\left(\dfrac{y}{x}\right) = 0$, given that $y = \dfrac{\pi}{2}$, when $x = 1$.

15. Show that following diff. eq. is homogeneous, and then solve it

$\left(xe^{y/x} + y\right)dx = xdy$, given that $y = 1$, when $x = 1$.

16. Show that following diff. eq. is homogeneous, and then solve it

$\left[x\sin^2\left(\dfrac{y}{x}\right) - y\right]dx + xdy = 0$, given that $y = \dfrac{\pi}{4}$, when $x = 1$.

ANSWERS

1. $x^2 + y^2 = 2x$

2. $\log\left(\dfrac{2y^2 - xy + x^2}{x^2}\right) + \dfrac{6}{\sqrt{7}}\tan^{-1}\left(\dfrac{4y - x}{\sqrt{7}\,x}\right) + 2\log x = \log 2 + \dfrac{6}{\sqrt{7}}\tan^{-1}\left(\dfrac{3}{\sqrt{7}}\right)$

3. $x\log\left(x^3 y\right) = C$

4. $\cos\dfrac{y}{x} = \log x + 1$

5. $x\sin\dfrac{y}{x} = C$

6. $-\dfrac{x^3}{3y^3} + \log|y| = C$

7. $3x^2 y = y + 2x$

8. $\log\left|x^2 + xy + y^2\right| - 2\sqrt{3}\tan^{-1}\left(\dfrac{2y + x}{\sqrt{3}x}\right) = C$

9. $\left[\log\dfrac{y}{x} - 1\right] = Cy$

10. $y + \sqrt{x^2 + y^2} = Cx^2$

11. $\dfrac{2x}{y} = \log|x| + C$

12. $\left(\text{cosec}\dfrac{y}{x} - \cot\dfrac{y}{x}\right) = 2$

13. $2e^{x/y} + \log|y| = C$

14. $\cos\dfrac{y}{x} = \log|x|$

15. $e^{\frac{y}{x}}.\log|x| - e^{\frac{y}{x}-1} + 1 = 0$

16. $\log|x| - \cot\dfrac{y}{x} + 1 = 0$

LINEAR DIFFERENTIAL EQUATIONS

Solve the following differential equations :

1. Solve $\cos^2 x\dfrac{dy}{dx} + y = \tan x$

2. Solve $x\dfrac{dy}{dx} + y = x\log x$; $x \neq 0$

3. Solve $(1+x^2)\dfrac{dy}{dx} + y = \tan^{-1} x$

4. Solve $x \log x \dfrac{dy}{dx} + y = 2\log x$

5. Solve : $\dfrac{dy}{dx} + y = \cos x - \sin x$

6. Solve : $\dfrac{dy}{dx} + y\cot x = 4x\,\mathrm{cosec}\,x,\ (x \neq 0),$ given that $y\left(\dfrac{\pi}{2}\right) = 0.$

7. Solve : $(x^2 - 1)\dfrac{dy}{dx} + 2xy = \dfrac{2}{x^2 - 1}$

8. Solve : $x\log x \dfrac{dy}{dx} + y = \dfrac{2}{x}\log x$

9. Solve : $(x^2 + 1)\dfrac{dy}{dx} + 2xy = \sqrt{x^2 + 4}$

10. Solve : $x\,dy + (y - x^3)dx = 0$

11. Solve : $\dfrac{dy}{dx} + 2y\tan x = \sin x;\ y\left(\dfrac{\pi}{3}\right) = 0$

12. Solve : $(1+x^2)dy + 2xy\,dx = \cot x\,dx\ ;\ x \neq 0$

13. Solve : $(1+x^2)\dfrac{dy}{dx} + y = e^{\tan^{-1} x}$

14. Solve : $\left[\dfrac{e^{-2\sqrt{x}}}{\sqrt{x}} - \dfrac{y}{\sqrt{x}}\right]\dfrac{dx}{dy} = 1$

ANSWERS

1. $ye^{\tan x} = e^{\tan x}\left(\tan x - 1\right) + C$

2. $y = \dfrac{x}{2}\left(\log x - \dfrac{1}{2}\right) + C$

3. $y = (\tan^{-1} x - 1) + Ce^{-\tan^{-1} x}$

4. $y\log x = \left(\log x\right)^2 + C$

5. $y = \cos x + Ce^{-x}$

6. $y\sin x = 2x^2 - \dfrac{\pi^2}{2}$

7. $y = \dfrac{1}{x^2 - 1}\log\left|\dfrac{x-1}{x+1}\right| + \dfrac{C}{x^2 - 1}$

8. $y\log x = -\dfrac{2}{x}\left[\log x + 1\right] + C$

9. $(x^2 + 1)y = \dfrac{x}{2}\sqrt{x^2 + 4} + 2\log\left|x + \sqrt{x^2 + 4}\right| + C$

10. $xy = \dfrac{x^4}{4} + C$

11. $y = \cos x - 2\cos^2 x$

12. $y = \dfrac{\log\sin x}{1 + x^2} + \dfrac{C}{1 + x^2}$

13. $y = \dfrac{e^{\tan^{-1} x}}{2} + Ce^{-\tan^{-1} x}$

14. $y.e^{2\sqrt{x}} = 2\sqrt{x} + C$

VECTORS
SOME IMPORTANT RESULTS/CONCEPTS

* Position vector of point $A(x, y, z) = \overrightarrow{OA} = x\hat{i} + y\hat{j} + z\hat{k}$

* If $A(x_1, y_1, z_1)$ and point $B(x_2, y_2, z_2)$ then $\overrightarrow{AB} = (x_2 - x_1)\hat{i} + (y_2 - y_1)\hat{j} + (z_2 - z_1)\hat{k}$

* If $\vec{a} = x\hat{i} + y\hat{j} + z\hat{k}$; $\left|\vec{a}\right| = \sqrt{x^2 + y^2 + z^2}$

* Unit vector parallel to $\vec{a} = \dfrac{\vec{a}}{\left|\vec{a}\right|}$

* Scalar Product (dot product) between two vectors : $\vec{a}.\vec{b} = \left|\vec{a}\right|\left|\vec{b}\right|\cos\theta$; θ is angle between the vectors

* $\cos\theta = \dfrac{\vec{a}.\vec{b}}{\left|\vec{a}\right|\left|\vec{b}\right|}$

* If $\vec{a} = a_1\hat{i} + b_1\hat{j} + c_1\hat{k}$ and $\vec{b} = a_2\hat{i} + b_2\hat{j} + c_2\hat{k}$ then $\vec{a}.\vec{b} = a_1a_2 + b_1b_2 + c_1c_2$

* If $\vec{a}$ is perpendicular to $\vec{b}$ then $\vec{a}.\vec{b} = 0$

* $\vec{a}.\vec{a} = \left|\vec{a}\right|^2$

* Projection of $\vec{a}$ on $\vec{b} = \dfrac{\vec{a}.\vec{b}}{\left|\vec{b}\right|}$

* Vector product between two vectors:

  $\vec{a} \times \vec{b} = \left|\vec{a}\right|\left|\vec{b}\right|\sin\theta\ \hat{n}$; $\hat{n}$ is the normal unit vector

  which is perpendicular to both $\vec{a}$ & $\vec{b}$

* $\hat{n} = \dfrac{\vec{a} \times \vec{b}}{\left|\vec{a} \times \vec{b}\right|}$

* If $\vec{a}$ is parallel to $\vec{b}$ then $\vec{a} \times \vec{b} = 0$

* Area of triangle (whose sides are given by $\vec{a}$ and $\vec{b}$) $= \dfrac{1}{2}\left|\vec{a} \times \vec{b}\right|$

* Area of parallelogram (whose adjacent sides are given by $\vec{a}$ and $\vec{b}$) $= \left|\vec{a} \times \vec{b}\right|$

* Area of parallelogram (whose diagonals are given by $\vec{a}$ and $\vec{b}$) $= \dfrac{1}{2}\left|\vec{a} \times \vec{b}\right|$

SOME ILUSTRATIONS :

Q. If $\vec{a} + \vec{b} + \vec{c} = 0$ and $|\vec{a}| = 3$, $|\vec{b}| = 5$ and $|\vec{c}| = 7$, show) that angle between $\vec{a}$ and $\vec{b}$ is 60°.

Sol. $\vec{a} + \vec{b} + \vec{c} = 0 \Rightarrow \vec{a} + \vec{b} = -\vec{c} \Rightarrow (\vec{a} + \vec{b})^2 = (-\vec{c})^2$

$$\Rightarrow (\vec{a} + \vec{b}) . (\vec{a} + \vec{b}) = \vec{c} . \vec{c}$$

$$\Rightarrow |\vec{a}|^2 + |\vec{b}|^2 + 2\vec{a} . \vec{b} = |\vec{c}|^2$$

$$\Rightarrow 9 + 25 + 2\vec{a} . \vec{b} = 49$$

$$\Rightarrow 2\vec{a} . \vec{b} = 15 \Rightarrow 2|\vec{a}||\vec{b}| \cos\theta = 15$$

$$\Rightarrow 2 \times 3 \times 5 \cos\theta = 15 \Rightarrow \cos\theta = \frac{1}{2}$$

$$\Rightarrow \theta = 60^{\circ}.$$

SHORT ANSWER TYPE QUESTIONS

1. Write two different vectors having same magnitude.

2. Write two different vectors having same direction.

3. Write down a unit vector in XY-plane, making an angle of 30° with the positive direction of x-axis.

4. Find the scalar and vector components of the vector with initial point (2, 1, 3) and terminal point (– 5, 7, 7).

5. Find the unit vector in the direction of the vector $\vec{a} = \hat{i} + 2\hat{j} + 2\hat{k}$.

6. Find the unit vector in the direction of vector $\vec{PQ}$, where P and Q are the points (2, 3, 4) and (5, 6, 7), respectively.

7. For given vectors, $\vec{a} = 3\hat{i} - \hat{j} + 2\hat{k}$ and $\vec{b} = -2\hat{i} + 3\hat{j} - \hat{k}$, find the unit vector in the direction of the vector $\vec{a} + \vec{b}$.

8. Find a vector of magnitude 4 units, and parallel to the resultant of the vectors $\vec{a} = 3\hat{i} + 2\hat{j} - \hat{k}$ and $\vec{b} = \hat{i} + 2\hat{j} + 3\hat{k}$.

9. Find a vector in the direction of vector $3\hat{i} - 4\hat{j} + 5\hat{k}$ which has magnitude 7 units.

10. Find the value of x for which $x(\hat{i} + 2\hat{j} + 3\hat{k})$ is a unit vector.

11. Find the value of λ for which the vectors $2\hat{i} - 3\hat{j} + 4\hat{k}$ and $-4\hat{i} + 6\hat{j} - \lambda\hat{k}$ are collinear.

12. Find the angle between the vectors $\vec{a} = \hat{i} - \hat{j} + \hat{k}$ and $\vec{b} = \hat{i} + \hat{j} - \hat{k}$

13. Write a unit vector in the direction of vector $\vec{PQ}$, where P and Q are the points (1, 3, 0) and (4, 5, 6) respectively.

14. What is the cosine of the angle which the vector $\sqrt{2}\hat{i} + \hat{j} + \hat{k}$ makes with y - axis?

15. Find the projection of the vector $\hat{i} + 3\hat{j} + 7\hat{k}$ on the vector $2\hat{i} - 3\hat{j} + 6\hat{k}$

16. Write the projection of vector $\hat{i} + \hat{j} + \hat{k}$ along the vector $\hat{j}$.

17. Find 'λ' when the projection of $\vec{a} = \lambda\hat{i} + \hat{j} + 4\hat{k}$ on $\vec{b} = 2\hat{i} + 6\hat{j} + 3\hat{k}$ is 4 units.

18. Find the position vector of a point R which divides the line joining two points P and Q whose position vectors are $\hat{i} + 2\hat{j} - \hat{k}$ and $-\hat{i} + \hat{j} + \hat{k}$ respectively, internally in the ratio 2 : 1

19. In a triangle OAC, if B is the mid-point of side AC and $\vec{OA} = \vec{a}$, $\vec{OB} = \vec{b}$, then what is $\vec{OC}$.

20. The two vectors $\hat{j}+\hat{k}$ and $3\hat{i}-\hat{j}+4\hat{k}$ represent the two sides AB and AC, respectively of a $\triangle ABC$. Find the length of the median through A.

21. Write the value of p for which $\vec{a}=3\hat{i}+2\hat{j}+9\hat{k}$ and $\vec{b}=\hat{i}+p\hat{j}+3\hat{k}$ are parallel vectors.

22. If θ is the angle between two vectors $\vec{a}$ and $\vec{b}$, then write the values of θ for which $\vec{a}\cdot\vec{b}\geq0$.

23. Find the projection of $\vec{a}$ on $\vec{b}$ if $\vec{a}\cdot\vec{b}=8$ and $\vec{b}=2\hat{i}+6\hat{j}+3\hat{k}$.

24. If $|\vec{a}|=\sqrt{3}$, $|\vec{b}|=2$ and $\vec{a}\cdot\vec{b}=\sqrt{3}$, find the angle between $\vec{a}$ and $\vec{b}$.

25. If $|\vec{a}|=\sqrt{3}$, $|\vec{b}|=2$ and the angle between $\vec{a}$ and $\vec{b}$ is $60°$, find $\vec{a}\cdot\vec{b}$.

26. For what value of λ are the vectors $\vec{a}=2\hat{i}+\lambda\hat{j}+\hat{k}$ and $\vec{b}=\hat{i}-2\hat{j}+3\hat{k}$ perpendicular to each other?

27. If $\vec{a}\cdot\vec{a}=0$ and $\vec{a}\cdot\vec{b}=0$, then what can be concluded about the vector $\vec{b}$?

28. If $\vec{a}$ is a unit vector and $(\vec{x}-\vec{a})\cdot(\vec{x}+\vec{a})=80$, then find $|\vec{x}|$.

29. If $\vec{a}$ is a unit vector and $(2\vec{x}-3\vec{a})\cdot(2\vec{x}+3\vec{a})=91$, then write the value of $|\vec{x}|$.

30. If $\vec{a}$ and $\vec{b}$ are perpendicular vectors, $|\vec{a}+\vec{b}|=13$ and $|\vec{a}|=5$, find the value of $|\vec{b}|$.

31. Write the value of $(\hat{i}\times\hat{j})\cdot\hat{k}+\hat{i}\cdot\hat{j}$.

32. Write the value of $(\hat{k}\times\hat{j})\cdot\hat{i}+\hat{j}\cdot\hat{k}$.

33. Write the value of $(\hat{i}\times\hat{j})\cdot\hat{k}+(\hat{j}\times\hat{k})\cdot\hat{i}$.

34. If $\vec{a}$ and $\vec{b}$ are two vectors such that $|\vec{a}\cdot\vec{b}|=|\vec{a}\times\vec{b}|$, then what is the angle between $\vec{a}$ and $\vec{b}$?

35. Write a unit vector perpendicular to both the vectors $\vec{a}=\hat{i}+\hat{j}+\hat{k}$ and $\vec{b}=\hat{i}+\hat{j}$

36. Find a vector of magnitude $\sqrt{171}$ which is perpendicular to both of the vectors $\vec{a}=\hat{i}+2\hat{j}-3\hat{k}$ and $\vec{b}=3\hat{i}-\hat{j}+2\hat{k}$

37. If vectors $\vec{a}$ and $\vec{b}$ are such that, $|\vec{a}|=3$, $|\vec{b}|=\dfrac{2}{3}$ and $\vec{a}\times\vec{b}$ is a unit vector, then write the angle between $\vec{a}$ and $\vec{b}$.

38. For any three vectors $\vec{a}$, $\vec{b}$ and $\vec{c}$, write the value of the following:

$\vec{a}\times(\vec{b}+\vec{c})+\vec{b}\times(\vec{c}+\vec{a})+\vec{c}\times(\vec{a}+\vec{b})$.   0

39. Vectors $\vec{a}$ and $\vec{b}$ are such that $|\vec{a}|=\sqrt{3}$, $|\vec{b}|=\dfrac{2}{3}$ and $(\vec{a}\times\vec{b})$ is a unit vector. Write the angle between $\vec{a}$ and $\vec{b}$.

40. Find the angle between two vectors $\vec{a}$ and $\vec{b}$, with magnitudes 1 and 2 respectively and when $|\vec{a}\times\vec{b}|=\sqrt{3}$

41. Find $\vec{a}\cdot(\vec{b}\times\vec{c})$, if $\vec{a}=2\hat{i}+\hat{j}+3\hat{k}$, $\vec{b}=-\hat{i}+2\hat{j}+\hat{k}$ and $\vec{c}=3\hat{i}+\hat{j}+2\hat{k}$

42. Find a vector $\overrightarrow{a}$ of magnitude $5\sqrt{2}$, making an angle of $\dfrac{\pi}{4}$ with x-axis, $\dfrac{\pi}{2}$ with y-axis and an acute angle θ with z-axis.

43. Find the value of p, if $(2\hat{i} + 6\hat{j} + 27\hat{k}) \times (\hat{i} + 3\hat{j} + p\hat{k}) = \overrightarrow{0}$

44. If $\overrightarrow{a}$ and $\overrightarrow{b}$ are two unit vectors such that $\overrightarrow{a} + \overrightarrow{b}$ is also a unit vector, then find the angle between $\overrightarrow{a}$ and $\overrightarrow{b}$.

45. If $\hat{a}$, $\hat{b}$ and $\hat{c}$ are mutually perpendicular unit vectors, then find the value of $|2\hat{a} + \hat{b} + \hat{c}|$.

46. If $|\overrightarrow{a}| = a$, then find the value of the following : $|\overrightarrow{a} \times \hat{i}|^2 + |\overrightarrow{a} \times \hat{j}|^2 + |\overrightarrow{a} \times \hat{k}|^2$.

47. Find the area of a parallelogram whose adjacent sides are represented by the vectors $2\hat{i} - 3\hat{k}$ and $4\hat{j} + 2\hat{k}$

48. Find the value of $\overrightarrow{a} \cdot \overrightarrow{b}$ if $|\overrightarrow{a}| = 10$, $|\overrightarrow{b}| = 2$ and $|\overrightarrow{a} \times \overrightarrow{b}| = 16$.

49. If $\overrightarrow{a}$ and $\overrightarrow{b}$ are unit vectors, then what is the angle between $\overrightarrow{a}$ and $\overrightarrow{b}$ so that $\sqrt{2}\overrightarrow{a} - \overrightarrow{b}$ is a unit vector ?

50. The vectors $\overrightarrow{a} = 3\hat{i} + x\hat{j}$ and $\overrightarrow{b} = 2\hat{i} + \hat{j} + y\hat{k}$ are mutually perpendicular. If $|\overrightarrow{a}| = |\overrightarrow{b}|$, then find the value of y.

51. If $|\overrightarrow{a}| = 4$, and $|\overrightarrow{b}| = 3$ and $\overrightarrow{a} \cdot \overrightarrow{b} = 6\sqrt{3}$, then find the value of $|\overrightarrow{a} \times \overrightarrow{b}|$.

52. If vectors and are such that $|\overrightarrow{a}| = \dfrac{1}{2}$, $|\overrightarrow{b}| = \dfrac{4}{\sqrt{3}}$ and $|\overrightarrow{a} \times \overrightarrow{b}| = \dfrac{1}{\sqrt{3}}$, then find $|\overrightarrow{a} \cdot \overrightarrow{b}|$.

53. Find the volume of the parallelopiped whose adjacent edges are represented by $2\overrightarrow{a}$, $-\overrightarrow{b}$ and $3\overrightarrow{c}$, where $\overrightarrow{a} = \hat{i} - \hat{j} + 2\hat{k}$ r, $\overrightarrow{b} = 3\hat{i} + 4\hat{j} - 5\hat{k}$ and $\overrightarrow{c} = 2\hat{i} - \hat{j} + 3\hat{k}$

ANSWERS

1. $2\hat{i} + 3\hat{j}$ and $3\hat{i} + 2\hat{j}$

2. $\hat{i} + \hat{j} + \hat{k}$ and $2\hat{i} + 2\hat{j} + 2\hat{k}$

3. $\dfrac{\sqrt{3}}{2}\hat{i} + \dfrac{1}{2}\hat{j}$

4. Scalar components : –7, 6 and 4,   Vector components : $-7\hat{i}$, $6\hat{j}$, and $4\hat{k}$.

5. $\dfrac{1}{3}(\hat{i} + 2\hat{j} + 2\hat{k})$

6. $\dfrac{1}{\sqrt{3}}(\hat{i} + \hat{j} + \hat{k})$

7. $\dfrac{1}{\sqrt{6}}(\hat{i} + \hat{j} + \hat{k})$

8. $\pm\dfrac{2}{3}(4\hat{i} + 4\hat{j} + 2\hat{k})$

9. $\dfrac{7}{5\sqrt{2}}(3\hat{i} - 4\hat{j} + 5\hat{k})$

10. $\pm\dfrac{1}{\sqrt{14}}(\hat{i} + 2\hat{j} + 3\hat{k})$

11. $\lambda = 8$

12. $\cos^{-1}\left(-\dfrac{1}{3}\right)$

13. $\frac{1}{7}(3\hat{i}+2\hat{j}+6\hat{k})$

14. $\frac{1}{2}$

15. 5

16. 1

17. 5

18. $-\frac{1}{3}\hat{i}+\frac{4}{3}\hat{j}+\frac{1}{3}\hat{k}$

19. $2\vec{b}-\vec{a}$

20. $\frac{1}{2}\sqrt{34}$

21. $p=\frac{2}{3}$

22. $0\le\theta\le\frac{\pi}{2}$

23. $\frac{8}{7}$

24. $\frac{\pi}{3}$

25. $\sqrt{3}$

26. $\lambda=\frac{5}{2}$

27. $\vec{b}$ may be any vector.

28. 9

29. 5

30. 12

31. 1

32. -1

33. 2

34. $\frac{\pi}{4}$

35. $-\frac{\hat{i}}{\sqrt{2}}+\frac{\hat{j}}{\sqrt{2}}$

36. $\hat{i}-11\hat{j}-7\hat{k}$

37. $\frac{\pi}{6}$

38. 0

39. $\frac{\pi}{3}$

40. $\frac{\pi}{3}$

41. -10

42. $5\hat{i}+5\hat{k}$

43. $\frac{27}{2}$

44. $\frac{2\pi}{3}$

45. $\sqrt{6}$

46. $2a^2$

47. $4\sqrt{14}$ sq units

48. ± 12

49. $\frac{\pi}{4}$

50. $\pm 2\sqrt{10}$

51. 6

52. 1

53. 24

LONG ANSWER TYPE QUESTIONS

1. If $\hat{i}+\hat{j}+\hat{k}$, $2\hat{i}+5\hat{j}$, $3\hat{i}+2\hat{j}-3\hat{k}$ and $\hat{i}-6\hat{j}-\hat{k}$ are the position vectors of the points A, B, C and D, find the angle between $\overrightarrow{AB}$ and $\overrightarrow{CD}$. Deduce that $\overrightarrow{AB}$ and $\overrightarrow{CD}$ are collinear.

2. If $\vec{a}=\hat{i}+\hat{j}+\hat{k}$ and $\vec{b}=\hat{j}-\hat{k}$ find a vector $\vec{c}$ such that $\vec{a}\times\vec{c}=\vec{b}$ and $\vec{a}.\vec{c}=3$.

3. If $\vec{a}+\vec{b}+\vec{c}=0$ and $|\vec{a}|=3$, $|\vec{b}|=5$ and $|\vec{c}|=7$, show that angle between $\vec{a}$ and $\vec{b}$ is 60°

4. The scalar product of the vector $\hat{i} + \hat{j} + \hat{k}$ with a unit vector along the sum of the vectors $2\hat{i} + 4\hat{j} - 5\hat{k}$ and $\lambda\hat{i} + 2\hat{j} + 3\hat{k}$ is equal to 1, find the value of λ.

5. If $\vec{a} \times \vec{b} = \vec{c} \times \vec{d}$ and $\vec{a} \times \vec{c} = \vec{b} \times \vec{d}$, show that $\vec{a} - \vec{d}$ is parallel to $\vec{b} - \vec{c}$, where $\vec{a} \neq \vec{d}$ and $\vec{b} \neq \vec{c}$.

6. If $\vec{a}$, $\vec{b}$, $\vec{c}$ are three vectors such that $\vec{a} \cdot \vec{b} = \vec{a} \cdot \vec{c}$ and $\vec{a} \times \vec{b} = \vec{a} \times \vec{c}$, $\vec{a} \neq 0$, then show that $\vec{b} = \vec{c}$.

7. If $\vec{a} = \hat{i} + \hat{j} + \hat{k}$, $\vec{b} = 4\hat{i} - 2\hat{j} + 3\hat{k}$, $\vec{c} = \hat{i} - 2\hat{j} + \hat{k}$ find a vector of magnitude 6 units which is parallel to the vector $2\vec{a} - \vec{b} + 3\vec{c}$.

8. Let $\vec{a} = \hat{i} + 4\hat{j} + 2\hat{k}$, $\vec{b} = 3\hat{i} - 2\hat{j} + 7\hat{k}$ and $\vec{c} = 2\hat{i} - \hat{j} + 4\hat{k}$ Find a vector $\vec{d}$ which is perpendicular to both $\vec{a}$ and $\vec{b}$ and $\vec{c} \cdot \vec{d} = 18$.

9. Let $\vec{a} = \hat{i} - \hat{j}$, $\vec{b} = 3\hat{j} - \hat{k}$ and $\vec{c} = 7\hat{i} - \hat{k}$. Find a vector $\vec{d}$ which is perpendicular to both $\vec{a}$ and $\vec{b}$ and $\vec{c} \cdot \vec{d} = 1$.

10. Find the position vector of a point R which divides the line joining two points P and Q whose position vectors are $(2\vec{a} + \vec{b})$ and $(\vec{a} - 3\vec{b})$ respectively, externally in the ratio 1 : 2. Also, show that P is the mid-point of the line segment RQ.

11. If the scalar product of the vector $\hat{i} + 2\hat{j} + 4\hat{k}$ with a unit vector along the sum of the vectors $\hat{i} + 2\hat{j} + 3\hat{k}$ and $\lambda\hat{i} + 4\hat{j} - 3\hat{k}$ is equal to one, find the value of λ.

12. If two vectors $\vec{a}$ and $\vec{b}$ are such that $|\vec{a}| = 2$, $|\vec{b}| = 1$ and $\vec{a} \cdot \vec{b} = 1$, then find the value of $(3\vec{a} - 5\vec{b}) \cdot (2\vec{a} + 7\vec{b})$.

13. If $\vec{a}$, $\vec{b}$, $\vec{c}$ are three vectors such that $|\vec{a}| = 5$, $|\vec{b}| = 12$ and $|\vec{c}| = 13$, $\vec{a} + \vec{b} + \vec{c} = 0$, find the value of $\vec{a} \cdot \vec{b} + \vec{b} \cdot \vec{c} + \vec{c} \cdot \vec{a}$.

14. The magnitude of the vector product of the vector $\hat{i} + \hat{j} + \hat{k}$ with a unit vector along the sum of vectors $2\hat{i} + 4\hat{j} - 5\hat{k}$ and $\lambda\hat{i} + 2\hat{j} + 3\hat{k}$ is equal to 2. Find the value of λ.

15. Vectors $\vec{a}$, $\vec{b}$ and $\vec{c}$ are such that $\vec{a} + \vec{b} + \vec{c} = 0$ and $|\vec{a}| = 3$, $|\vec{b}| = 5$ and $|\vec{c}| = 7$. Find the angle between $\vec{a}$ and $\vec{b}$.

16. Find a unit vector perpendicular to each of the vectors $\vec{a} + \vec{b}$ and $\vec{a} - \vec{b}$, where $\vec{a} = 3\hat{i} + 2\hat{j} + 2\hat{k}$ and $\vec{b} = \hat{i} + 2\hat{j} - 2\hat{k}$.

17. If vectors $\vec{a} = 2\hat{i} + 2\hat{j} + 3\hat{k}$, $\vec{b} = -\hat{i} + 2\hat{j} + \hat{k}$ and $\vec{c} = 3\hat{i} + \hat{j}$ are such that $\vec{a} + \lambda\vec{b}$ is perpendicular to $\vec{c}$, then find the value of λ.

18. If $\vec{\alpha} = 3\hat{i} + 4\hat{j} + 5\hat{k}$ and $\vec{\beta} = 2\hat{i} + \hat{j} - 4\hat{k}$, then express $\vec{\beta}$ in the form $\vec{\beta} = \vec{\beta_1} + \vec{\beta_2}$, where $\vec{\beta_1}$ is parallel to $\vec{\alpha}$ and $\vec{\beta_2}$ is perpendicular to $\vec{\alpha}$.

19. If $\vec{\alpha} = 3\hat{i} - \hat{j}$ and $\vec{\beta} = 2\hat{i} + \hat{j} - 3\hat{k}$, then express $\vec{\beta}$ in the form $\vec{\beta} = \vec{\beta_1} + \vec{\beta_2}$, where $\vec{\beta_1}$ is parallel to $\vec{\alpha}$ and $\vec{\beta_2}$ is perpendicular to $\vec{\alpha}$.

20. The two adjacent sides of a parallelogram are $2\hat{i} - 4\hat{j} + 5\hat{k}$ and $\hat{i} - 2\hat{j} - 3\hat{k}$. Find the unit vector parallel to one of its diagonals. Also, find its area.

21. If $\vec{a} = \hat{i} - \hat{j} + 7\hat{k}$ and $\vec{b} = 5\hat{i} - \hat{j} + \lambda\hat{k}$, then find the value of λ, so that $\vec{a} + \vec{b}$ and $\vec{a} - \vec{b}$ are perpendicular vectors.

22. Using vectors, find the area of the triangle ABC, whose vertices are A (1, 2, 3), B (2, –1, 4) and C (4, 5, –1).

23. If $\vec{a}$ and $\vec{b}$ are two vectors such that $|\vec{a} + \vec{b}| = |\vec{a}|$, then prove that vector $2\vec{a} + \vec{b}$ perpendicular

to vector $\vec{b}$.

24. Find a vector of magnitude 6, perpendicular to each of the vectors $\vec{a} + \vec{b}$ and $\vec{a} - \vec{b}$, where

$\vec{a} = \hat{i} + \hat{j} + \hat{k}$ and $\vec{b} = \hat{i} + 2\hat{j} + 3\hat{k}$.

25. Find a unit vector perpendicular to each of the vectors $\vec{a} + 2\vec{b}$ and $2\vec{a} + \vec{b}$, where $\vec{a} = 3\hat{i} + 2\hat{j} + 2\hat{k}$ and $\vec{b} = \hat{i} + 2\hat{j} - 2\hat{k}$.

26. Find a unit vector perpendicular to the plane of triangle ABC, where the coordinates of its vertices are A(3, – 1, 2), B(1, – 1, – 3) and C(4, – 3, 1).

27. If $\vec{r} = x\hat{i} + y\hat{j} + z\hat{k}$, find $(\vec{r} \times \hat{i}) \cdot (\vec{r} \times \hat{j}) + xy$

28. Dot product of a vector with $\hat{i} + \hat{j} - 3\hat{k}$, $\hat{i} + 3\hat{j} - 2\hat{k}$, and $2\hat{i} + \hat{j} + 4\hat{k}$ are 0, 5, 8 respectively. Find the vector.

29. If $\vec{a}$ & $\vec{b}$ are unit vectors inclined at an angle θ, prove that

(i) $\sin\dfrac{\theta}{2} = \dfrac{1}{2}|\vec{a} - \vec{b}|$ (ii) $\tan\dfrac{\theta}{2} = \dfrac{|\vec{a} - \vec{b}|}{|\vec{a} + \vec{b}|}$.

30. If $\vec{a}$, $\vec{b}$, $\vec{c}$ are three mutually perpendicular vectors of equal magnitudes, prove that $\vec{a} + \vec{b} + \vec{c}$ is equally inclined with the vectors $\vec{a}$, $\vec{b}$, $\vec{c}$.

31. Let $\vec{a}$, $\vec{b}$, $\vec{c}$ be unit vectors such that $\vec{a} \cdot \vec{b} = \vec{a} \cdot \vec{c} = 0$ and the angle between $\vec{b}$ and $\vec{c}$ is $\pi/6$, prove that $\vec{a} = \pm 2(\vec{a} \times \vec{b})$.

32. If $\vec{a}$, $\vec{b}$, $\vec{c}$, $\vec{d}$ are four distinct vectors satisfying the conditions $\vec{a} \times \vec{b} = \vec{c} \times \vec{d}$ and $\vec{a} \times \vec{c} = \vec{b} \times \vec{d}$, then prove that $\vec{a} \cdot \vec{b} + \vec{c} \cdot \vec{d} \ne \vec{a} \cdot \vec{c} + \vec{b} \cdot \vec{d}$.

33. Find the angles which the vector $\vec{a} = \hat{i} - \hat{j} + \sqrt{2}\hat{k}$ makes with the coordinate axes.

ANSWERS

1. $\overrightarrow{AB} \parallel \overrightarrow{CD}$

2. $\dfrac{1}{3}(5\hat{i} + 2\hat{j} + 2\hat{k})$

4. 1

7. $2\hat{i} - 4\hat{j} + 4\hat{k}$

8. $64\hat{i} - 2\hat{j} - 28\hat{k}$

9. $\dfrac{1}{4}(\hat{i} + \hat{j} + 3\hat{k})$

10. $\overrightarrow{OR} = 3\vec{a} + 5\vec{b}$

11. 8

12. 0

13. -169

14. 1

15. $60°$

16. $\pm \dfrac{2}{3}\hat{i} \mp \dfrac{2}{3}\hat{j} \mp \dfrac{1}{3}\hat{k}$

17. 8

18. $\left(-\dfrac{3}{5}\hat{i} - \dfrac{4}{5}\hat{j} - \hat{k}\right) + \left(\dfrac{13}{5}\hat{i} + \dfrac{9}{5}\hat{j} - 3\hat{k}\right)$

19. $\left(\dfrac{3}{2}\hat{i} - \dfrac{1}{2}\hat{j}\right) + \left(\dfrac{1}{2}\hat{i} + \dfrac{3}{2}\hat{j} - 3\hat{k}\right)$

20. $3\hat{i} - 6\hat{j} + 2\hat{k}$, $11\sqrt{5}$ sq. units

21. ± 5

22. $\dfrac{\sqrt{274}}{2}$ Sq units

24. $\pm\sqrt{6}(-\hat{i} + 2\hat{j} - \hat{k})$

25. $\pm \dfrac{2}{3}(\hat{i} - \hat{j} - \hat{k})$

26. $\pm \dfrac{1}{\sqrt{165}}(-10\hat{i} - 7\hat{j} + 4\hat{k})$

27. 0

28. $\hat{i} + 2\hat{j} + \hat{k}$

33. $\dfrac{\pi}{3}, \dfrac{2\pi}{3}, \dfrac{\pi}{4}$

THREE DIMENSIONAL GEOMETRY
SOME IMPORTANT RESULTS/CONCEPTS

** Direction cosines and direction ratios:

If a line makes angles α, β and γ with x, y and z axes respectively the $\cos\alpha$, $\cos\beta$ and $\cos\gamma$ are the direction cosines denoted by l, m, n respectively and $l^2 + m^2 + n^2 = 1$

Any three numbers proportional to direction cosines are direction ratios denoted by a, b, c

$$\frac{l}{a} = \frac{m}{b} = \frac{n}{c} \qquad l = \pm\frac{a}{\sqrt{a^2+b^2+c^2}}, \quad m = \pm\frac{b}{\sqrt{a^2+b^2+c^2}}, \quad n = \pm\frac{c}{\sqrt{a^2+b^2+c^2}},$$

* Direction ratios of a line segment joining $P(x_1, y_1, z_1)$ and $Q(x_2, y_2, z_2)$ may be taken as $x_2 - x_1, \ y_2 - y_1, \ z_2 - z_1$

* Angle between two lines whose direction cosines are l_1, m_1, n_1 and l_2, m_2, n_2 is given by

$$\cos\theta = l_1 l_2 + m_1 m_2 + n_1 n_2 = \frac{a_1 a_2 + b_1 b_2 + c_1 c_2}{\sqrt{\left(a_1^2 + b_1^2 + c_1^2\right)\left(a_2^2 + b_2^2 + c_2^2\right)}}$$

* For parallel lines $\dfrac{a_1}{a_2} = \dfrac{b_1}{b_2} = \dfrac{c_1}{c_2}$ and

for perpendicular lines $a_1 a_2 + b_1 b_2 + c_1 c_2 = 0$ or $l_1 l_2 + m_1 m_2 + n_1 n_2 = 0$

** STRAIGHT LINE :

* Equation of line passing through a point (x_1, y_1, z_1) with direction cosines a, b, c: $\dfrac{x-x_1}{a} = \dfrac{y-y_1}{b} = \dfrac{z-z_1}{c}$

* Equation of line passing through a point (x_1, y_1, z_1) and parallel to the line: $\dfrac{x-\alpha}{a} = \dfrac{y-\beta}{b} = \dfrac{z-\gamma}{c}$ is

$$\frac{x-x_1}{a} = \frac{y-y_1}{b} = \frac{z-z_1}{c}$$

* Equation of line passing through two point (x_1, y_1, z_1) and (x_2, y_2, z_2) is $\dfrac{x-x_1}{x_2-x_1} = \dfrac{y-y_1}{y_2-y_1} = \dfrac{z-z_1}{z_2-z_1}$

* Equation of line (Vector form)

Equation of line passing through a point $\vec{a}$ and in the direction of $\vec{b}$ is $\vec{r} = \vec{a} + \lambda\vec{b}$

* Equation of line passing through two points $\vec{a}$ & $\vec{b}$ and in the direction of $\vec{b}$ is $\vec{r} = \vec{a} + \lambda(\vec{b} - \vec{a})$

* Shortest distance between two skew lines : if lines are $\vec{r} = \vec{a_1} + \lambda\vec{b_1}$ $\vec{r} = \vec{a_2} + \lambda\vec{b_2}$

then Shortest distance $= \dfrac{(\vec{a_2} - \vec{a_1})(\vec{b_1} \times \vec{b_2})}{\left|\vec{b_1} \times \vec{b_2}\right|}$ $\ ; \vec{b_1} \times \vec{b_2} \neq 0$

$$\frac{\left|(\vec{a_2} - \vec{a_1}) \times \vec{b_1}\right|}{\left|\vec{b_1}\right|} \qquad ; \vec{b_1} \times \vec{b_2} = 0$$

SOME ILUSTRATIONS :

Q. Find the shortest distance between the following lines :

$$\frac{x-3}{1} = \frac{y-5}{-2} = \frac{z-7}{1} \quad \text{and} \quad \frac{x+1}{7} = \frac{y+1}{-6} = \frac{z+1}{1}$$

Sol. Given lines are $\vec{r} = (3\hat{i} + 5\hat{j} + 7\hat{k}) + \lambda(\hat{i} - 2\hat{j} + \hat{k})$, and

$\vec{r} = (-\hat{i} - \hat{j} - \hat{k}) + \mu(7\hat{i} - 6\hat{j} + \hat{k})$ $\vec{r} = (-\hat{i} - \hat{j} - \hat{k}) + \mu(7\hat{i} - 6\hat{j} + \hat{k})$

$\vec{a_1} = 3\hat{i} + 5\hat{j} + 7\hat{k}, \ \vec{b_1} = \hat{i} - 2\hat{j} + \hat{k};$

71

$$\vec{a_2} = -\hat{i} - \hat{j} - \hat{k}, \quad \vec{b_2} = 7\hat{i} - 6\hat{j} + \hat{k}$$

$$\vec{a_2} - \vec{a_1} = -4\hat{i} - 6\hat{j} - 8\hat{k}, \quad \vec{b_1} \times \vec{b_2} = \begin{vmatrix} \hat{i} & \hat{j} & \hat{k} \\ 1 & -2 & 1 \\ 7 & -6 & 1 \end{vmatrix} = 4\hat{i} + 6\hat{j} + 8\hat{k}$$

$$S.D. = \frac{\left|(\vec{a_2} - \vec{a_1}).(\vec{b_1} \times \vec{b_2})\right|}{\left|\vec{b_1} \times \vec{b_2}\right|} = \frac{\left|(-4\hat{i} - 6\hat{j} - 8\hat{k}).(4\hat{i} + 6\hat{j} + 8\hat{k})\right|}{\left|4\hat{i} + 6\hat{j} + 8\hat{k}\right|}$$

$$= \frac{|-16 - 36 - 64|}{\sqrt{16 + 36 + 64}} = \frac{116}{\sqrt{116}} = \sqrt{116} = 2\sqrt{29}$$

Q. Show that the lines $\dfrac{x+1}{3} = \dfrac{y+3}{5} = \dfrac{z+5}{7}$ and $\dfrac{x-2}{1} = \dfrac{y-4}{3} = \dfrac{z-6}{5}$ intersect. Find their point of intersection.

Sol. Any point on $\dfrac{x+1}{3} = \dfrac{y+3}{5} = \dfrac{z+5}{7} = \lambda$ is $(3\lambda - 1, 5\lambda - 3, 7\lambda - 5)$

Any point on $\dfrac{x-2}{1} = \dfrac{y-4}{3} = \dfrac{z-6}{5} = \mu$ is $(\mu + 2, 3\mu + 4, 5\mu + 6)$

If the lines intersect than for some λ & μ

$$3\lambda - 1 = \mu + 2 \qquad \Rightarrow 3\lambda - \mu = 3 \text{.......(i)}$$
$$5\lambda - 3 = 3\mu + 4 \qquad \Rightarrow 5\lambda - 3\mu = 7 \text{.......(ii)}$$
$$7\lambda - 5 = 5\mu + 6 \qquad \Rightarrow 7\lambda - 5\mu = 11 \text{.....(iii)}$$

From (i) & (ii) $\lambda = \dfrac{1}{2}$, $\mu = -\dfrac{3}{2}$ which satisfies (iii)

$\Rightarrow$ given lines intersect and point of intersection is $\left(\dfrac{1}{2}, -\dfrac{1}{2}, -\dfrac{3}{2}\right)$

SHORT ANSWER TYPE QUESTIONS

1. Find the direction cosines of the line passing through the two points $(1, -2, 4)$ and $(-1, 1, -2)$.

2. Find the direction cosines of x, y and z-axis.

3. If a line makes angles $90°, 135°, 45°$ with the x, y and z axes respectively, find its direction cosines.

4. Find the acute angle which the line with direction-cosines $\left\langle \dfrac{1}{\sqrt{3}}, \dfrac{1}{\sqrt{6}}, n \right\rangle$ makes with positive direction of z-axis.

5. Find the length of the perpendicular drawn from the point $(4, -7, 3)$ on the y-axis.

6. Find the coordinates of the foot of the perpendicular drawn from the point $(2, -3, 4)$ on the y-axis.

7. Find the coordinates of the foot of the perpendicular drawn from the point $(-2, 8, 7)$ on the XZ-plane.

8. Find the image of the point $(2, -1, 4)$ in the YZ-plane.

9. Find the vector and cartesian equations for the line passing through the points $(1, 2, -1)$ and $(2, 1, 1)$.

10. Find the vector equation of a line passing through the point $(2, 3, 2)$ and parallel to the line

$$\vec{r} = (-2\hat{i} + 3\hat{j}) + \lambda(2\hat{i} - 3\hat{j} + 6\hat{k}).$$

11. Find the angle between the lines $\vec{r} = (2\hat{j} - 3\hat{k}) + \lambda(\hat{i} + 2\hat{j} + 2\hat{k})$ and

$\vec{r} = (2\hat{i} + 6\hat{j} + 3\hat{k}) + \lambda(2\hat{i} + 3\hat{j} - 6\hat{k})$.

12. The two lines $x = ay + b$, $z = cy + d$; and $x = a' y + b'$, $z = c' y + d'$ are perpendicular to each other, find the relation involving a, a', c and c'.

13. If the two lines $L_1 : x = 5, \dfrac{y}{3-\alpha} = \dfrac{z}{-2}$, $L_2 : x = 2, \dfrac{y}{-1} = \dfrac{z}{2-\alpha}$ are perpendicular, then find value of α.

14. Find the vector equation of the line passing through the point $(-1, 5, 4)$ and perpendicular to the plane $z = 0$.

ANSWERS

1. $\left(-\dfrac{2}{7}, \dfrac{3}{7}, -\dfrac{6}{7}\right)$

2. 1, 0, 0; 0, 1, 0 and 0, 0, 1

3. $0, -\dfrac{1}{\sqrt{2}}, \dfrac{1}{\sqrt{2}}$

4. $\dfrac{\pi}{4}$

5. 5 units

6. $(0, -3, 0)$

7. $(-2, 0, 7)$

8. $(-2, -1, 4)$

9. $\vec{r} = (\hat{i} + 2\hat{j} - \hat{k}) + \mu(\hat{i} - \hat{j} + 2\hat{k}); \dfrac{x-1}{1} = \dfrac{x-2}{-1} = \dfrac{z+1}{2}$

10. $\vec{r} = (-2\hat{i} + 3\hat{j} + 2\hat{k}) + \mu(2\hat{i} - 3\hat{j} + 6\hat{k})$

11. $\cos^{-1}\left(\dfrac{4}{\sqrt{21}}\right)$

12. aa' + cc' = 1

13. $\dfrac{7}{3}$

14. $\vec{r} = -\hat{i} + 5\hat{j} + (4 + \lambda)\hat{k}$

LONG ANSWER TYPE QUESTIONS

1. Find the shortest distance between the lines $\vec{r} = (\hat{i} + 2\hat{j} + \hat{k}) + \lambda(\hat{i} - \hat{j} + \hat{k})$ and

$\vec{r} = 2\hat{i} - \hat{j} - \hat{k} + \mu(2\hat{i} + \hat{j} + 2\hat{k})$

2. Find the shortest distance between the following lines : $\dfrac{x-3}{1} = \dfrac{y-5}{-2} = \dfrac{z-7}{1}$ and $\dfrac{x+1}{7} = \dfrac{y+1}{-6} = \dfrac{z+1}{1}$

3. Find the equation of a line parallel to

$\vec{r} = (\hat{i} + 2\hat{j} + 3\hat{k}) + \lambda(2\hat{i} + 3\hat{j} + 4\hat{k})$ and passing through $2\hat{i} + 4\hat{j} + 5\hat{k}$. Also find the S.D. between these lines.

4. Find the equation of the line passing through $(1, -1, 1)$ and perpendicular to the lines joining the points $(4, 3, 2)$, $(1, -1, 0)$ and $(1, 2, -1)$, $(2, 2, 1)$.

5. Find the value of λ so that the lines $\dfrac{1-x}{3} = \dfrac{y-2}{2\lambda} = \dfrac{z-3}{2}$ and $\dfrac{x-1}{3\lambda} = \dfrac{y-1}{1} = \dfrac{6-z}{7}$ are perpendicular to each other.

6. Show that the lines $\dfrac{x+1}{3} = \dfrac{y+3}{5} = \dfrac{z+5}{7}$ and $\dfrac{x-2}{1} = \dfrac{y-4}{3} = \dfrac{z-6}{5}$ intersect. Find their point of intersection.

7. Find the image of the point $(1, 6, 3)$ in the line $\dfrac{x}{1} = \dfrac{y-1}{2} = \dfrac{z-2}{3}$.

8. Find the point on the line $\dfrac{x+2}{3} = \dfrac{y+1}{2} = \dfrac{z-3}{2}$ at a distance 5 units from the point P(1, 3, 3).

9. Find the shortest distance between the following lines and hence write whether the lines are intersecting or not. $\dfrac{x-1}{2} = \dfrac{y-1}{3} = z$, $\dfrac{x+1}{5} = \dfrac{y-2}{1}$, $z = 2$.

10. A line with direction ratios $< 2, 2, 1 >$ intersects the lines $\dfrac{x-3}{7} = \dfrac{y-5}{2} = \dfrac{z-3}{1}$ and $\dfrac{x-1}{2} = \dfrac{y+1}{4} = \dfrac{z+1}{3}$ at the points P and Q respectively. Find the length and the equation of the intercept PQ.

ANSWERS

1. $\dfrac{3\sqrt{2}}{2}$ units

2. $2\sqrt{29}$ units

3. $\dfrac{\sqrt{5}}{\sqrt{29}}$ or $\dfrac{\sqrt{145}}{29}$ units

4. $\dfrac{x-1}{2} = \dfrac{y+1}{1} = \dfrac{z-1}{-1}$

5. $\lambda = -2$

6. $\left(\dfrac{1}{2}, -\dfrac{1}{2}, -\dfrac{3}{2}\right)$

7. $(1, 0, 7)$

8. $(-2, -1, 3)$ or $(4, 3, 7)$

9. $\dfrac{9}{\sqrt{195}}$, lines are not intersecting.

10. Length 3 units and the equation $\dfrac{x-1}{2} = \dfrac{y-1}{2} = \dfrac{z-1}{1}$

LINEAR PROGRAMMING

** **An Optimisation Problem** A problem which seeks to maximise or minimise a function is called an optimisation problem. An optimisation problem may involve maximisation of profit, production etc or minimisation of cost, from available resources etc.

** **Linnear Programming Problem (LPP)**

A linear programming problem deals with the optimisation (maximisation/minimisation) of a **linear function** of two variables (say x and y) known as **objective function** subject to the conditions that the variables are non-negative and satisfy a set of linear inequalities (called **linear constraints**). A linear programming problem is a special type of optimisation problem.

** **Objective Function** Linear function Z = ax + by, where a and b are constants, which has to be maximised or minimised is called a linear objective function.

** **Decision Variables** In the objective function Z = ax + by, x and y are called decision variables.

** **Constraints** The linear inequalities or restrictions on the variables of an LPP are called **constraints**. The conditions x ≥ 0, y ≥ 0 are called non-negative constraints.

** **Feasible Region** The common region determined by all the constraints including non-negative constraints x ≥ 0, y ≥ 0 of an LPP is called the feasible region for the problem.

** **Feasible Solutions** Points within and on the boundary of the feasible region for an LPP represent feasible solutions.

** **Infeasible Solutions** Any Point outside feasible region is called an infeasible solution.

** **Optimal (feasible) Solution** Any point in the feasible region that gives the optimal value (maximum or minimum) of the objective function is called an optimal solution.

** Let R be the feasible region (convex polygon) for an LPP and let Z = ax + by be the objective function. When Z has an optimal value (maximum or minimum), where x and y are subject to constraints described by linear inequalities, this optimal value must occur at a corner point (vertex) of the feasible region.

** Let R be the feasible region for a LPP and let Z = ax + by be the objective function. If R is **bounded**, then the objective function Z has both a maximum and a minimum value on R and each of these occur at a corner point of R. If the feasible region R is **unbounded**, then a maximum or a minimum value of the objective function may or may not exist. However, if it exits, it must occur at a corner point of R.

SHORT ANSWER TYPE QUESTIONS

1. Find the maximum value of the objective function Z = 5x + 10 y subject to the constraints
   x + 2y ≤ 120, x + y ≥ 60, x − 2y ≥ 0, x ≥ 0, y ≥ 0.

2. Find the maximum value of Z = 3x + 4y subjected to constraints x + y ≤ 40, x+ 2y ≤ 60, x ≥ 0 and y ≥ 0.

3. Find the points where the minimum value of Z occurs:
   Z = 6x + 21 y, subject to x + 2y ≥ 3, x + 4y ≥ 4, 3x + y ≥ 3, x ≥ 0, y ≥ 0.

4. For the following feasible region, write the linear constraints.

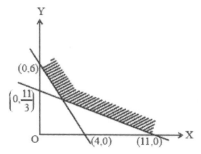

5. The feasible region for LPP is shown shaded in the figure. Let $Z = 3x - 4y$ be the objective function, then write the maximum value of Z.

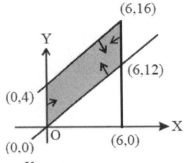

6. Feasible region for an LPP is shown shaded in the following figure. Find the point where minimum of $Z = 4x + 3y$ occurs.

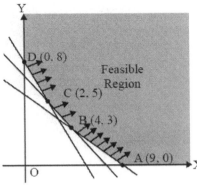

7. Write the linear inequations for which the shaded area in the Following figure is the solution set.

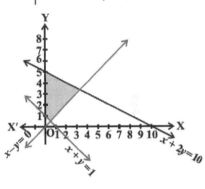

8. Write the linear inequations for which the shaded area in the following figure is the solution set.

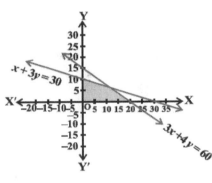

9. Write the linear inequations for which the shaded area in the following figure is the solution set.

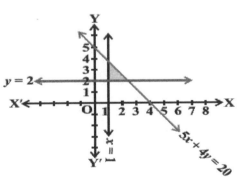

10. Solve the following Linear Programming Problems graphically: Maximise $Z = 5x + 3y$ subject to $3x + 5y \leq 15$, $5x + 2y \leq 10$, $x \geq 0$, $y \geq 0$.

76

ANSWERS

1. 600

2. 140

3. (2 , 72)

4. $x \geq 0$, $y \geq 0$, $3x + 2y \geq 12$, $x + 3y \geq 11$

5. 0

6. (0, 8)

7. $x + 2y \leq 10$, $x + y \geq 1$, $x - y \leq 0$, $x, y \geq 0$

8. $3x + 4y \leq 60$, $x + 3y \leq 30$, $x \geq 0$, $y \geq 0$

9. $5x + 4y \leq 20$, $x \geq 1$, $y \geq 2$

10. Maximum $Z = \dfrac{235}{19}$ at $\left(\dfrac{20}{19}, \dfrac{45}{19} \right)$

PROBABILITY
SOME IMPORTANT RESULTS/CONCEPTS

** Sample Space and Events :

The set of all possible outcomes of an experiment is called the sample space of that experiment. It is usually denoted by S. The elements of S are called events and a subset of S is called an event.

ϕ ($\subset$ S) is called an impossible event and

S($\subset$ S) is called a sure event.

** Probability of an Event.

(i) If E be the event associated with an experiment, then probability of E, denoted by P(E) is

defined as $P(E) = \dfrac{\text{number of outcomes in E}}{\text{number of total outcomes in sample space S}}$

it being assumed that the outcomes of the experiment in reference are equally likely.

(ii) P(sure event or sample space) = P(S) = 1 and P(impossible event) = P(ϕ) = 0.

(iii) If E_1, E_2, E_3, ... ,E_k are mutually exclusive and exhaustive events associated with an experiment

(i.e. if $E_1 \cup E_2 \cup E_3 \cup .... \cup E_k$) = S and $E_i \cap E_j = \phi$ for i, j $\in$ {1, 2, 3,.....,k} i$\neq$ j), then

$P(E_1) + P(E_2) + P(E_3) + ...+ P(E_k) = 1$.

(iv) $P(E) + P(E^C) = 1$

** If E and F are two events associated with the same sample space of a random experiment, the conditional probability of the event E given that F has occurred, i.e. P (E|F) is given by

$P(E|F) = \dfrac{P(E \cap F)}{P(F)}$ provided $P(F) \neq 0$

** Multiplication rule of probability : $P(E \cap F) = P(E)\, P(F|E)$

$= P(F)\, P(E|F)$ provided $P(E) \neq 0$ and $P(F) \neq 0$.

** Independent Events :E and F are two events such that the probability of occurrence of one of them is not affected by occurrence of the other.

Let E and F be two events associated with the same random experiment, then E and F are said to be independent if $P(E \cap F) = P(E) \cdot P(F)$.

** Bayes' Theorem :If E_1, E_2 ,..., E_n are n non empty events which constitute a partition of sample space S, i.e. E_1, E_2 ,..., E_n are pairwise disjoint and $E_1 \cup E_2 \cup ... \cup E_n$= S and A is any event of nonzero probability, then

$P(Ei|A) = \dfrac{P(E_i).P(A|E_i)}{\displaystyle\sum_{j=1}^{n} P(E_j) P(A|E_j)}$ for any i = 1, 2, 3, ..., n

** The probability distribution of a random variable X is the system of numbers

X :	x_1	x_2	...	x_n
P(X) :	p_1	p_2	...	p_n

where, $p_i > 0$, $\displaystyle\sum_{i=1}^{n} p_i = 1$, i = 1, 1, 2,...,

** Binomial distribution: The probability of x successes P (X = x) is also denoted by P (x) and is given by $P(x) = {}^nC_x q^{n-x} p^x$, x = 0, 1,..., n. (q = 1 – p)

SOME ILUSTRATIONS :

Q. A factory has two machines A and B. Past record shows that machine A produced 60% of the items of output and machine B produced 40% of the items. Further, 2% of the items produced by machine A and 1% produced by machine B were defective. All the items are put into one stockpile and then one item is chosen at random from this and is found to be defective. What is the probability that was produced by machine B?

Sol. Let E_1 and E_2 be the respective events of items produced by machines A and B and X be the event that the produced item was found to be defective.

$$\therefore P(E_1) = 60\% = \frac{3}{5} , \quad P(E_2) = 40\% = \frac{2}{5}$$

$$P(X|E_1) = 2\% = \frac{2}{100} , \quad P(X|E_2) = 1\% = \frac{1}{100}$$

$$P(E_2|X) = \frac{P(E_2) \cdot P(X|E_2)}{P(E_1) \cdot P(X|E_1) + P(E_2) \cdot P(X|E_2)}$$

$$= \frac{\dfrac{2}{5} \cdot \dfrac{1}{100}}{\dfrac{3}{5} \cdot \dfrac{2}{100} + \dfrac{2}{5} \cdot \dfrac{1}{100}} = \frac{\dfrac{2}{500}}{\dfrac{6}{500} + \dfrac{2}{500}}$$

$$= \frac{1}{4}$$

Q : Suppose a girl throws a die. If she gets a 5 or 6, she tosses a coin three times and notes the number of heads. If she gets 1, 2, 3 or 4, she tosses a coin once and notes whether a head or tail is obtained. If she obtained exactly one head, what is the probability that she threw 1, 2, 3 or 4 with the die?

Sol. Let E_1 be the event that the outcome on the die is 5 or 6 and E_2 be the event that the outcome on the die is 1, 2, 3, or 4.

$$\therefore P(E_1) = \frac{2}{6} = \frac{1}{3} \text{ and } P(E_2) = \frac{4}{6} = \frac{2}{3}$$

Let A be the event of getting exactly one head.

$$P(A|E_1) = \frac{3}{8} , \quad P(A|E_2) = \frac{1}{2}$$

$$P(E_2|A) = \frac{P(E_2) \cdot P(A|E_2)}{P(E_1) \cdot P(A|E_1) + P(E_2) \cdot P(A|E_2)}$$

$$= \frac{\dfrac{2}{3} \cdot \dfrac{1}{2}}{\dfrac{1}{3} \cdot \dfrac{3}{8} + \dfrac{2}{3} \cdot \dfrac{1}{2}} = \frac{\dfrac{1}{3}}{\dfrac{1}{3}\left(\dfrac{3}{8} + 1\right)} = \frac{8}{11}$$

SHORT ANSWER TYPE QUESTIONS

1. If P(A) = 0·6, P(B) = 0·5 and P(B|A) = 0·4, find P(A ∪ B) and P(A|B).
2. Evaluate P(A ∪ B), if 2P(A) = P(B) =5/13 and P(A/B) = 2/5.
3. If P(not A) = 0·7, P(B) = 0·7 and P(B/A) = 0·5, then find P(A/B).
4. Mother, father and son line up at random for a family photo. If A and B are two events given by
   A = Son on one end, B = Father in the middle, find P(B/A).

5. A black die and a red die are rolled together. Find the conditional probability of obtaining a sum greater than 9 given that the black die resulted in a 5.

6. A card is picked at random from a pack of 52 playing cards. Given that the picked card is a queen, find the probability of this card to be a card of spade.

7. Given that the two numbers appearing on throwing two dice are different, find the probability of the event 'the sum of numbers on the dice is 10'.

8. A die marked 1, 2, 3 in red and 4, 5, 6 in green is tossed. Let A be the event "number is even" and B be the event "number is marked red". Find whether the events A and B are independent or not.

9. A die is thrown twice and the sum of the numbers appearing is observed to be 6. What is the conditional probability that the number 4 has appeared at least once?

10. A die is thrown three times. Events A and B are defined as below:

A : 4 on the third throw, B : 6 on the first and 5 on the second throw.

Find the probability of A given that B has already occurred.

11. Assume that each born child is equally likely to be a boy or a girl. If a family has two children, what is the conditional probability that both are girls given that (i) the youngest is a girl, (ii) at least one is a girl?

12. Given that the two numbers appearing on throwing two dice are different. Find the probability of the event 'the sum of numbers on the dice is 4'.

13. If A and B are two independent events and $P(A) = \dfrac{1}{3}$ and $P(B) = \dfrac{1}{2}$, find $P(\overline{A} \mid \overline{B})$.

14. If A and B are two independent events with $P(A) = 1/3$ and $P(B) = 1/4$, then $P(B' \mid A)$ is equal to

15. Given two independent events A and B such that $P(A) = 0.3$ and $P(B) = 0.6$, find $P(A' \cap B')$. Ans.

16. If A and B are two events such that $P(A) = 0.4$, $P(B) = 0.3$ and $P(A \cup B) = 0.6$, then find $P(B' \cap A)$.

17. Two cards are drawn at random and without replacement from a pack of 52 playing cards. Find the probability that both the cards are spades.

18. Three cards are drawn successively, without replacement from a pack of 52 well shuffled cards. What is the probability that first two cards are aces and the third card drawn is a king?

19. Two balls are drawn at random with replacement from a box containing 10 black and 8 red balls. Find the probability that one of them is black and other is red.

20. A die is tossed thrice. Find the probability of getting an even number at least once.

21. A coin is tossed once. If head comes up, a die is thrown, but if tail comes up, the coin is tossed again.

Find the probability of obtaining head and number 6.

22. Two cards are drawn successively without replacement from a well-shuffled pack of 52 cards. Find the probability of getting one king and one non-king.

23. From a pack of 52 cards, 3 cards are drawn at random (without replacement). Find the probability that they are two red cards and one black card.

24. A bag contains 3 black, 4 red and 2 green balls. If three balls are drawn simultaneously at random. Find the probability that the balls are of different colours .

25. The probability of solving a specific question independently by A and B are $\dfrac{1}{3}$ and $\dfrac{1}{5}$ respectively. If both try to solve the question independently, what is the probability that the question is solved.

26. A problem is given to three students whose probabilities of solving it are $\dfrac{1}{3}, \dfrac{1}{4}$ and $\dfrac{1}{6}$ respectively.

If the events of solving the problem are independent, find the probability that at least one of them solves it.

27. The probability distribution of X is:

X	0	1	2	3
P(X)	0.2	k	k	2k

Write the value of k.

28. A random variable X has the following probability distribution:

X:	0	1	2	3	4	5	6	7
P(X):	0	k	2k	2k	3k	k^2	$2k^2$	$7k^2 + k$

Determine k .

29. The random variable X has a probability distribution P(X) of the following form, where k is some

number : $P(X) = \begin{cases} k, & \text{if } x = 0 \\ 2k, & \text{if } x = 1 \\ 3k, & \text{if } x = 2 \\ 0, & \text{otherwise} \end{cases}$ .Find P (X < 2)

30. Let X represents the difference between the number of heads and the number of tails obtained when a coin is tossed 6 times. What are possible values of X?

ANSWERS

1. $P(A \cup B) = 0.86$, $P(A|B) = 0.48$.　**2.** $\dfrac{11}{26}$　**3.** $\dfrac{5}{16}$

4. $\dfrac{1}{2}$　**5.** $\dfrac{1}{3}$　**6.** $\dfrac{1}{4}$

7. $\dfrac{1}{15}$　**8.** A and B are not independent.　**9.** $\dfrac{2}{5}$

10. $\dfrac{1}{6}$　**11.** (i) $\dfrac{1}{2}$ (ii) $\dfrac{1}{3}$　**12.** $\dfrac{1}{15}$

13. $\dfrac{2}{3}$　**14.** $\dfrac{3}{4}$　**15.** 0.28

16. 0.3　**17.** $\dfrac{1}{17}$　**18.** $\dfrac{2}{5525}$

19. $\dfrac{40}{81}$　**20.** $\dfrac{7}{8}$　**21.** $\dfrac{1}{12}$.

22. $\dfrac{32}{221}$.　**23.** $\dfrac{13}{34}$　**24.** $\dfrac{2}{7}$

25. $\dfrac{7}{15}$　**26.** $\dfrac{7}{12}$　**27.** 0.2

28 $\dfrac{1}{10}$　**29.** $\dfrac{1}{2}$　**30.** 0, 2,4

LONG ANSWER TYPE QUESTIONS

1. There are two groups of bags. The first group has 3 bags, each containing 5 red and 3 black balls. The second group has 2 bags, each containing 2 red and 4 black balls. A ball is drawn at random from one of the bags and is found to be red. Find the probability that this ball is from a bag of first group.

2. A bag contains 5 red and 3 black balls and another bag contains 2 red and 6 black balls. Two balls are drawn at random (without replacement) from one of the bags and both are found to be red. Find the probability that balls are drawn from the first bag.

3. Of the students in a school, it is known that 30% have 100% attendance and 70% students are irregular. Previous year results report that 70% of all students who have 100% attendance attain A grade and 10% irregular students attain A grade in their annual examination. At the end of the year, one student is chosen at random from the school and he was found to have an A grade. What is the probability that the student has 100% attendance ?

4. A bag contains two coins, one biased and the other unbiased. When tossed, the biased coin has a 60% chance of showing heads. One of the coins is selected at random and on tossing it shows tails. What is the probability it was an unbiased coin?

5. Suppose that 5 men out of 100 and 25 women out of 1000 are good orators. Assuming that there are equal number of men and women, find the probability of choosing a good orator.

6. A bag contains 4 red and 4 black balls, another bag contains 2 red and 6 black balls. One of the two bags is selected at random and a ball is drawn from the bag which is found to be red. Find the probability that the ball is drawn from the first bag.

7. Of the students in a college, it is known that 60% reside in hostel and 40% are day scholars (not residing in hostel). Previous year results report that 30% of all students who reside in hostel attain A grade and 20% of day scholars attain A grade in their annual examination. At the end of the year, one student is chosen at random from the college and he has an A grade, what is the probability that the student is hostler?

8. In answering a question on a multiple choice test, a student either knows the answer or guesses. Let 3/4 be the probability that he knows the answer and 1/4 be the probability that he guesses. Assuming that a student who guesses at the answer will be correct with probability 1/4 What is the probability that the student knows the answer given that he answered it correctly?

9. A girl throws a die. If she gets a 5 or 6, she tosses a coin three times and notes the number of heads. If she gets 1, 2, 3 or 4, she tosses a coin two times and notes the number of heads obtained. If she obtained exactly two heads, what is the probability that she threw 1, 2, 3 or 4 with the die?

10. A laboratory blood test is 99% effective in detecting a certain disease when it is in fact, present. However, the test also yields a false positive result for 0.5% of the healthy person tested (that is, if a healthy person is tested, then, with probability 0.005, the test will imply he has the disease). If 0.1 percent of the population actually has the disease, what is the probability that a person has the disease given that his test result is positive?

11. An insurance company insured 2000 scooter drivers, 4000 car drivers and 6000 truck drivers. The probability of accidents are 0.01, 0.03 and 0.15 respectively. One of the insured persons meets with an accident. What is the probability that he is a scooter driver?

12. A factory has two machines A and B. Past record shows that machine A produced 60% of the items of output and machine B produced 40% of the items. Further, 2% of the items produced by machine A and 1% produced by machine B were defective. All the items are put into one stockpile and then one item is chosen at random from this and is found to be defective. What is the probability that was produced by machine B?

13. Bag I contains 3 red and 4 black balls and Bag II contains 4 red and 5 black balls. One ball is transferred from Bag I to Bag II and then a ball is drawn from Bag II. The ball so drawn is found to be red in colour. Find the probability that the transferred ball is black.

14. Coloured balls are distributed in three bags as shown in the following table :

Bag	Colour of the ball		
	Black	White	Red
I	1	2	3
II	2	4	1
III	4	5	3

A bag is selected at random and then two balls are randomly drawn from the selected bag. They happen to be black and red. What is the probability that they came from bag I?

15. Three persons A, B and C apply for a job of manager in a private company. Chances of their selection (A, B and C) are in the ratio 1 : 2 : 4. The probabilities that A, B and C can introduce changes to improve profits of the company are 0.8, 0.5 and 0.3 respectively. If the change does not take place, find the probability that it is due to the appointment of C.

16. A bag contains 4 balls. Two balls are drawn at random (without replacement) and are found to be white. What is the probability that all balls in the bag are white?

17. A card from a pack of 52 cards is lost. From the remaining cards of the pack, two cards are drawn at random and are found to be both clubs. Find the probability of the lost card being of clubs.

18. In shop A, 30 tin pure ghee and 40 tin adulterated ghee are kept for sale while in shop B, 50 tin pure ghee and 60 tin adulterated ghee are there. One tin of ghee is purchased from one of the shops randomly and it is found to be adulterated. Find the probability that it is purchased from shop B.

19. Three machines E_1, E_2, E_3 in a certain factory produce 50%, 25% and 25% respectively, of the total daily output of electric tubes. It is known that 4% of the tube produced on each of machines E_1 and E_2 are defective and that 5% of those produced on E_3, are defective. If one tube is picked up at random from a day's production, calculate the probability that it is defective.

20. There are two boxes I and II. Box I contains 3 red and 6 black balls. Box II contains 5 red and 'n' black balls. One of the two boxes, box I and box II is selected at random and a ball is drawn at random. The ball drawn is found to be red. If the probability that this red ball comes out from box II is $\frac{3}{5}$, find the value of 'n'.

21. Bag I contains 3 red and 4 black balls and bag II contains 4 red and 5 black balls. Two balls are transferred at random from bag I to bag II and then a ball is drawn from bag II. The ball so drawn is found to be red in colour. Find the probability that the transferred balls were both black.

22. A bag contains 5 red and 3 black balls and another bag contains 2 red and 6 black balls. Two balls are drawn at random (without replacement) from one of the bags and both are found to be red. Find the probability that balls are drawn from first bag.

23. In a certain college, 4% of boys and 1% of girls are taller than 1.75 metres. Furthermore, 60% of the students in the college are girls. A student is selected at random from the college and is found to be taller than 1.75 metres. Find the probability that the selected student is a girl.

24. A and B throw a pair of dice alternately. A wins the game if he gets a total of 7 and B wins the game if he gets a total of 10. If A starts the game, then find the probability that B wins.

25. A and B throw a pair of dice alternately, till one of them gets a total of 10 and wins the game. Find their respective probabilities of winning, if A starts first.

26. A coin is biased so that the head is three times as likely to occur as tail. If the coin is tossed twice, find the probability distribution of number of tails. Hence find the mean of the number of tails.

27. A pair of dice is thrown 4 times. If getting a doublet is considered a success, find the probability distribution of number of successes.

28. Find the probability distribution of number of doublets in three throws of a pair of dice.

29. Two cards are drawn successively with replacement from a well-shuffled deck of 52 cards. Find the probability distribution of the number of kings.

30. Find the probability distribution of the number of successes in two tosses of a die, where a success is defined as **(i)** number greater than 4 **(ii)** six appears on at least one die.

31. A coin is biased so that the head is 3 times as likely to occur as tail. If the coin is tossed twice, find the probability distribution of number of heads.

ANSWERS

1. $\dfrac{45}{61}$

2. $\dfrac{10}{11}$

3. $\dfrac{3}{4}$

4. $\dfrac{5}{9}$

5. $\dfrac{3}{180}$

6. $\dfrac{2}{3}$

7. $\dfrac{9}{13}$

8. $\dfrac{12}{13}$

9. $\dfrac{8}{11}$

10. $\dfrac{22}{133}$

11. $\dfrac{1}{52}$

12. $\dfrac{1}{4}$

13. $\dfrac{16}{31}$

14. $\dfrac{231}{551}$

15. $\dfrac{7}{10}$

16. $\dfrac{3}{5}$

17. $\dfrac{11}{50}$

18. $\dfrac{21}{43}$

19. $\dfrac{17}{400}$

20. 5

21. $\dfrac{4}{17}$

22. $\dfrac{10}{11}$

23. $\dfrac{3}{11}$

24. $\dfrac{5}{17}$

25. $\dfrac{12}{23}, \dfrac{11}{23}$

26.

X	0	1	2
P(X)	$\dfrac{9}{16}$	$\dfrac{6}{16}$	$\dfrac{1}{16}$

27.

X	0	1	2	3	4
P(X)	$\dfrac{625}{1296}$	$\dfrac{500}{1296}$	$\dfrac{150}{1296}$	$\dfrac{20}{1296}$	$\dfrac{1}{1296}$

28

X	0	1	2	3
P(X)	$\dfrac{125}{216}$	$\dfrac{75}{216}$	$\dfrac{15}{216}$	$\dfrac{1}{216}$

29.

X	0	1	2
P(X)	$\dfrac{144}{169}$	$\dfrac{24}{169}$	$\dfrac{1}{169}$

30.(i)

X	1	1	2
P (X)	$\dfrac{4}{9}$	$\dfrac{4}{9}$	$\dfrac{1}{9}$

(ii)

Y	0	1
P (Y)	$\dfrac{25}{36}$	$\dfrac{11}{36}$

31.

X	0	1	2
P (X)	$\dfrac{9}{16}$	$\dfrac{3}{8}$	$\dfrac{1}{16}$

RELATIONS AND FUNCTIONS
Multiple Choice Questions [MCQ]

1. Let A = {1, 2, 3} and consider the relation R = {1, 1), (2, 2), (3, 3), (1, 2), (2, 3), (2,1)}. Then R is
(a) an equivalence relation
(b) reflexive and symmetric but not transitive
(c) reflexive and transitive but not symmetric
(d) reflexive but neither symmetric nor transitive

2. Let A = {1, 2, 3} and consider the relation R = {1, 1), (2, 2), (3, 3), (1, 2), (2, 3), (1,3), (3 , 1)}. Then R is
(a) an equivalence relation
(b) reflexive and symmetric but not transitive
(c) reflexive and transitive but not symmetric
(d) reflexive but neither symmetric nor transitive

3. Let A = {1, 2, 3} and consider the relation R = {1, 1), (2, 2), (3, 3), (1, 2), (2, 1)}.Then R is
(a) reflexive and symmetric but not transitive
(b) reflexive but neither symmetric nor transitive
(c) an equivalence relation
(d) reflexive and transitive but not symmetric

4. Let A = {1, 2, 3} and consider the relation R = {(1, 1), (1, 2), (2, 1)}. Then R is
(a) reflexive and symmetric but not transitive
(b) symmetric but neither reflexive nor transitive
(c) reflexive but neither symmetric nor transitive
(d) reflexive and transitive but not symmetric

5. Let A = {1, 2, 3} and consider the relation R = {(1, 3)}. Then R is
(a) transitive
(b) symmetric
(c) reflexive
(d) none of these

6. Let A = {1, 2, 3} and consider the relation R = {1, 1), (2, 2), (3, 3)}.Then R is
(a) reflexive and symmetric but not transitive
(b) reflexive but neither symmetric nor transitive
(c) reflexive and symmetric and transitive
(d) reflexive and transitive but not symmetric

7. Let A = {1, 2, 3} and R = {(1, 1), (2, 3), (1, 2)} be a relation on A, then the minimum number of ordered pairs to be added in **R** to make **R** reflexive and transitive.
(a) 4
(b) 2
(c) 3
(d) 1

8. The maximum number of equivalence relations on the set {1 , 2, 3} is
(a) 6
(b) 4
(c) 3
(d) 5

9. Let R be a relation on the set N be defined by {(x, y) : x, y ∈ N, 2x + y = 41}. Then, R is
(a) reflexive
(b) symmetric
(c) transitive
(d) none of these

10. Relation R in the set **Z** of all integers defined as R = {(x, y) : x − y is an even integer}is
(a) reflexive and transitive
(b) symmetric and Transitive
(c) reflexive and symmetric
(d) an equivalence relation

11. Let R be the relation on the set of all real numbers defined by a R b iff |a − b| ≤ 1. Then, R is
(a) reflexive and transitive
(b) symmetric and Transitive
(c) reflexive and symmetric
(d) an equivalence relation

12. Consider the non-empty set consisting of children in a family and a relation R defined as aRb if a is sister of b. Then R is
(a) symmetric but not transitive
(b) transitive but not symmetric
(c) both symmetric and transitive
(d) neither symmetric nor transitive

13. Relation R in the set A = {1, 2, 3, 4, 5, 6, 7, 8} as R = {(x, y) : x divides y}is
(a) reflexive and symmetric but not transitive
(b) reflexive and transitive but not symmetric
(c) reflexive but neither symmetric nor transitive
(d) symmetric but neither reflexive nor transitive

14. Let L denote the set of all straight lines in a plane. Let a relation R be defined by l_1 R l_2 if and only if l_1 is perpendicular to l_2, $\forall l_1, l_2 \in L$. Then R is

(a) symmetric
(b) reflexive
(c) transitive
(d) reflexive and symmetric

15. If A = {a, b, c} then number of relations containing (a , b) and (a , c) which are reflexive and symmetric but not transitive is

(a) 4
(b) 3
(c) 2
(d) 1

16. The relation R in the set {1, 2, 3, ... , 13, 14} defined by R = {(x , y) : 3x − y = 0} is

(a) symmetric
(b) reflexive
(c) transitive
(d) none of these

17. The relation R in the set of natural numbers N defined by R = {(x , y) : x > y} is

(a) reflexive and symmetric but not transitive
(b) transitive but neither reflexive nor symmetric
(c) reflexive but neither symmetric nor transitive
(d) symmetric but neither reflexive nor transitive

18. A function f : X → Y is one-one (or injective), then which of the following is true?

(a) $\forall x_1, x_2 \in X, f(x_1) = f(x_2) \Rightarrow x_1 = x_2$.
(b) $x_1 \neq x_2 \Rightarrow f(x_1) \neq f(x_2)$.
(c) both (a) and (b) are true
(d) none of these

19. A function f : X → Y is said to be onto (or surjective), then which of the following is true?

(a) if $\forall y \in Y, \exists$ some $x \in X$ such that $y = f(x)$
(b) range of f = Y
(c) both (a) and (b) are true
(d) none of these

20. A function f : X → Y is said to be bijective , if f is

(a) one-one only
(b) onto only
(c) one-one but not onto
(d) one-one and onto

21. If a set A contains **m** elements and the set B contains **n** elements with n > m, then number of bijective functions from A to B will be:

(a) m × n
(b) m^n
(c) n^m
(d) 0

22. Which of the following functions from I(Set of Integers) to itself is a bijection?

(a) $f(x) = x^3$
(b) $f(x) = x + 2$
(c) $f(x) = 2x + 1$
(d) $f(x) = x^2 + x$

23. Let X = {− 1, 0, 1}, Y = {0, 2} and a function f : X → Y defined by $y = 2x^4$, is

(a) one-one onto
(b) one-one into
(c) many-one onto
(d) many-one into

24. Let $f(x) = x^2 − 4x − 5$, then

(a) f is one-one on R
(b) f is not one-one on R
(c) f is bijective on R
(d) None of these

25. The function f : R → R given by $f(x) = x^2$, x ∈ R when R is the set of real numbers, is

(a) one-one and onto
(b) onto but not one-one
(c) neither one-one nor onto
(d) one-one but not onto

26. The signum function, f : R → R is given by $f(x) = \begin{cases} 1, \text{if } x > 0 \\ 0, \text{if } x = 0 \\ -1, \text{if } x < 0 \end{cases}$

(a) one-one
(b) many-one
(c) onto
(d) none of these

27. Let $f : R \to R$ be defined by $f(x) = \begin{cases} 3x, & \text{if } x \le 1 \\ x^2, & \text{if } 1 < x \le 3 \\ 2x, & \text{if } x > 3 \end{cases}$, then $f(-1) + f(2) + f(4)$ is

(a) 9

(b) 3

(c) 4

(d) 8

28. The greatest integer function $f : R \to R$ be defined by $f(x) = [x]$ is

(a) one-one and onto

(b) onto but not one-one

(c) one-one but not onto

(d) neither one-one nor onto

29. The function $f : N \to N$, where N is the set of natural numbers is defined by

$$f(x) = \begin{cases} n^2, & \text{if } n \text{ is odd} \\ n^2 + 1, & \text{if } n \text{ is even} \end{cases}$$

(a) one-one and onto

(b) neither one-one nor onto

(c) one-one but not onto

(d) onto but not one-one

30. The total number of injective mappings from a set with m elements to a set with n elements, $m \le n$, is

(a) n^m

(b) m^n

(c) mn

(d) $\dfrac{n!}{(n-m)!}$

ANSWERS

Q. No.	1	2	3	4	5	6	7	8	9	10
Answer	(d)	(c)	(c)	(b)	(a)	(c)	(c)	(d)	(d)	(d)
Q. No.	11	12	13	14	15	16	17	18	19	20
Answer	(c)	(b)	(b)	(a)	(d)	(d)	(b)	(c)	(c)	(d)
Q. No.	21	22	23	24	25	26	27	28	29	30
Answer	(d)	(b)	(c)	(b)	(c)	(b)	(a)	(d)	(c)	(d)

INVERSE TRIGONOMETRIC FUNCTIONS
Multiple Choice Questions [MCQ]

1. Domain of $\sin^{-1}(2x-1)$ is

(a) $[-1, \ 1]$ (b) $[-1, \ 2]$

(c) $[1, \ 2]$ (d) $[-1, -2]$

2. Domain of $\sin^{-1}x + \cos x$ is

(a) $[-1, \ 1]$ (b) $[-1, \ 2]$

(c) $[1, \ 2]$ (d) $[-1, -2]$

3. Domain of $\sin^{-1}\sqrt{x-1}$ is

(a) $[-1, \ 1]$ (b) $[1, \ 2]$

(c) $[-1, \ 2]$ (d) $[-1, -2]$

4. Principal value of $\sec^{-1}(-2)$ is equal to

(a) $\dfrac{2\pi}{3}$ (b) $\dfrac{5\pi}{6}$

(c) $\dfrac{4\pi}{3}$ (d) $-\dfrac{2\pi}{3}$

5. Principal value of $\sin^{-1}\left(\cos\dfrac{2\pi}{3}\right)$ is equal to

(a) $-\dfrac{2\pi}{3}$ (b) $\dfrac{\pi}{6}$

(c) $-\dfrac{\pi}{6}$ (d) $\dfrac{2\pi}{3}$

6. Principal value of $\tan^{-1}\left(\tan\dfrac{15\pi}{4}\right)$ is equal to

(a) 1 (b) $-\dfrac{\pi}{4}$

(c) $\dfrac{15\pi}{4}$ (d) $\dfrac{\pi}{4}$

7. Principal value of $\sec^{-1}\left(2\sin\dfrac{3\pi}{4}\right)$ is equal to

(a) $\dfrac{\pi}{4}$ (b) $-\dfrac{\pi}{4}$

(c) $-\dfrac{3\pi}{4}$ (d) $\dfrac{3\pi}{4}$

8. Principal value of $\cot^{-1}\left(\tan\dfrac{3\pi}{4}\right)$ is equal to

(a) $-\dfrac{\pi}{4}$ (b) $\dfrac{\pi}{4}$

(c) $-\dfrac{3\pi}{4}$ (d) $\dfrac{3\pi}{4}$

9. Principal value of $\cos^{-1}\left(\cos\dfrac{3\pi}{2}\right)$ is equal to

(a) $\dfrac{3\pi}{2}$ 　　　　　　　　　　　　　　　　(b) $\dfrac{\pi}{2}$

(c) $-\dfrac{\pi}{2}$ 　　　　　　　　　　　　　　　(d) $-\dfrac{3\pi}{2}$

10 Principal value of $\sin^{-1}\left(\cos\dfrac{33\pi}{5}\right)$ is equal to

(a) $\dfrac{3\pi}{5}$ 　　　　　　　　　　　　　　　(b) $\dfrac{\pi}{10}$

(c) $-\dfrac{\pi}{10}$ 　　　　　　　　　　　　　　(d) $-\dfrac{3\pi}{5}$

11. Principal value of $\sin^{-1}\left(\sin\dfrac{3\pi}{5}\right)$ is equal to

(a) $\dfrac{2\pi}{5}$ 　　　　　　　　　　　　　　　(b) $\dfrac{3\pi}{5}$

(c) $-\dfrac{3\pi}{5}$ 　　　　　　　　　　　　　　(d) $-\dfrac{2\pi}{5}$

12. Principal value of $\cos^{-1}\left(\dfrac{\sqrt{3}+1}{2\sqrt{2}}\right)$ is equal to

(a) $\dfrac{7\pi}{12}$ 　　　　　　　　　　　　　　(b) $\dfrac{5\pi}{12}$

(c) $\dfrac{11\pi}{12}$ 　　　　　　　　　　　　　(d) $\dfrac{\pi}{12}$

13. The value of $\cos(\sin^{-1}x)$ is

(a) x 　　　　　　　　　　　　　　　　　(b) $\sqrt{1-x^2}$

(c) $\dfrac{\sqrt{1-x^2}}{x}$ 　　　　　　　　　　　(d) $\dfrac{x}{\sqrt{1-x^2}}$

14. The value of $\cot(\cos^{-1}x)$ is

(a) $\dfrac{x}{\sqrt{1+x^2}}$ 　　　　　　　　　　　(b) $\sqrt{1-x^2}$

(c) $\dfrac{\sqrt{1-x^2}}{x}$ 　　　　　　　　　　　(d) $\dfrac{x}{\sqrt{1-x^2}}$

15. The value of $\sin^{-1}\left\{\cos(\sin^{-1}\dfrac{\sqrt{3}}{2})\right\}$ is

(a) $\dfrac{\sqrt{3}}{2}$ 　　　　　　　　　　　　　(b) $-\dfrac{\pi}{6}$

(c) $\dfrac{\pi}{6}$ 　　　　　　　　　　　　　　　(d) $-\dfrac{\sqrt{3}}{2}$

16. The value of $\tan^{-1}\left\{2\cos\left(2\sin^{-1}\dfrac{1}{2}\right)\right\}$ is

(a) 1 　　　　　　　　　　　　　　　　　(b) $\dfrac{3\pi}{4}$

90

(c) $\dfrac{1}{2}$ (d) $\dfrac{\pi}{4}$

17. The value of $\cot\left[\sin^{-1}\left\{\cos\left(\tan^{-1}1\right)\right\}\right]$ is

(a) 1   (b) $\dfrac{3\pi}{4}$

(c) $\dfrac{1}{2}$ (d) $\dfrac{\pi}{4}$

18. The value of $\tan^{-1}\left\{2\sin\left(4\cos^{-1}\dfrac{\sqrt{3}}{2}\right)\right\}$ is

(a) $\dfrac{2\pi}{3}$ (b) $\dfrac{\pi}{3}$

(c) $\dfrac{\sqrt{3}}{2}$ (d) $\dfrac{\pi}{6}$

19. The value of $\cos^{-1}\left(\cos\dfrac{2\pi}{3}\right)+\sin^{-1}\left(\sin\dfrac{2\pi}{3}\right)$ is

(a) $\dfrac{2\pi}{3}$ (b) $\dfrac{4\pi}{3}$

(c) π (d) $\dfrac{\pi}{3}$

20. The value of $\tan^{-1}\left(\tan\dfrac{5\pi}{6}\right)+\cos^{-1}\left(\cos\dfrac{13\pi}{6}\right)$ is

(a) 0   (b) $\dfrac{5\pi}{6}$

(c) $\dfrac{13\pi}{6}$ (d) 3π

ANSWERS

Q. No.	1	2	3	4	5	6	7	8	9	10
Answer	(c)	(a)	(b)	(a)	(c)	(b)	(a)	(d)	(b)	(c)
Q. No.	11	12	13	14	15	16	17	18	19	20
Answer	(a)	(d)	(b)	(d)	(c)	(d)	(a)	(b)	(c)	(a)

1. Write the number of all possible matrices of order 2×2 with entries -1 or 0 or 1 ?
(a) 27
(b) 64
(c) 81
(d) 54

2. If a matrix has 12 elements, the number of possible orders it can have :
(a) 4
(b) 8
(c) 3
(d) 6

3. A matrix $A = \left[a_{ij} \right]_{3 \times 4}$, whose elements are given by $a_{ij} = \frac{1}{2} |i - 3j|^2$, then a_{32} is :

(a) $\dfrac{9}{2}$
(b) $\dfrac{9}{4}$

(c) $\dfrac{3}{2}$
(d) 2

4. If $\begin{bmatrix} 3x+7 & 5 \\ y+1 & 2-3x \end{bmatrix} = \begin{bmatrix} 2 & y-2 \\ 8 & 7 \end{bmatrix}$, then the values of x and y are :

(a) $x = -\dfrac{5}{3}, \ y = 5$
(b) $x = -\dfrac{5}{3}, \ y = 7$

(c) $x = \dfrac{5}{3}, \ y = 7$
(d) $x = -\dfrac{5}{3}, \ y = -7$

5. If $\begin{bmatrix} x+y & 2 \\ 5+z & xy \end{bmatrix} = \begin{bmatrix} 6 & 2 \\ 5 & 8 \end{bmatrix}$ the values of x, y and z are:
(a) x = 4, y = 2, z = 0 or x = 2, y = 4, z = 0
(b) x = –4, y = –2, z = 0 or x = 2, y = 4, z = 0
(c) x = 4, y = –2, z = 0 or x = 2, y = 4, z = 0
(d) x = 4, y = 2, z = 0 or x = 2, y = –4, z = 0

6. A matrix $A = [a_{ij}]_{m \times n}$ is called scalar matrix if :
(a) $a_{ij} = 0$ if $i \neq j$. and $a_{ij} = k$, $i = j$.
(b) where $a_{ij} \neq 0$ if $i \neq j$. and $a_{ij} = k$, $i = j$.
(c) $m \neq n$, $a_{ij} = 0$ if $i \neq j$. and $a_{ij} = k$, $i = j$.
(d) $m = n$, $a_{ij} = 0$ if $i \neq j$. and $a_{ij} = k$, $i = j$.

7. If $\begin{bmatrix} 1 & 2 \\ -2 & -b \end{bmatrix} + \begin{bmatrix} a & 4 \\ 3 & 2 \end{bmatrix} = \begin{bmatrix} 5 & 6 \\ 1 & 0 \end{bmatrix}$, then $a^2 + b^2 =$
(a) 12
(b) 21
(c) 20
(d) 22

8. If $3A - B = \begin{bmatrix} 5 & 0 \\ 1 & 1 \end{bmatrix}$ and $B = \begin{bmatrix} 4 & 3 \\ 2 & 5 \end{bmatrix}$, then the matrix $A =$

(a) $\begin{bmatrix} 3 & -1 \\ 1 & 2 \end{bmatrix}$
(b) $\begin{bmatrix} 3 & 1 \\ 1 & 2 \end{bmatrix}$

(c) $\begin{bmatrix} -3 & 1 \\ -1 & 2 \end{bmatrix}$
(d) $\begin{bmatrix} 3 & -1 \\ 1 & -2 \end{bmatrix}$

9. If A is a square matrix such that $A^2 = A$, then the simplified value of $(I - A)^3 + A$ is equal to
(a) A
(b) A^2
(c) I
(d) A^3

10. If A is a square matrix such that $A^2 = A$, then the simplified value of $(A - I)^3 + (A + I)^3 - 7A$ is equal to
(a) A
(b) A^3
(c) 3A
(d) I

11. If $\begin{bmatrix} 2 & 3 \\ 5 & 7 \end{bmatrix}\begin{bmatrix} 1 & -3 \\ -2 & 4 \end{bmatrix} = \begin{bmatrix} -4 & 6 \\ -9 & x \end{bmatrix}$, the value of x is

(a) 17   (b) 11

(c) 31   (d) 13

12. If $\begin{bmatrix} 1 & 0 & 0 \\ 0 & y & 0 \\ 0 & 0 & 1 \end{bmatrix}\begin{bmatrix} x \\ -1 \\ z \end{bmatrix} = \begin{bmatrix} 1 \\ 2 \\ 1 \end{bmatrix}$, then $x + y + z =$

(a) 1   (b) 0

(c) –1   (d) –2

13. For which value of x , $\begin{bmatrix} 1 & x & 1 \end{bmatrix}\begin{bmatrix} 1 & 2 & 3 \\ 4 & 5 & 6 \\ 3 & 2 & 5 \end{bmatrix}\begin{bmatrix} 1 \\ 2 \\ 3 \end{bmatrix} = [0]$?

(a) $\dfrac{9}{8}$ (b) $-\dfrac{11}{8}$

(c) $-\dfrac{9}{8}$ (d) $-\dfrac{8}{9}$

14. If $\begin{bmatrix} 2x & 3 \end{bmatrix}\begin{bmatrix} 1 & 2 \\ -3 & 0 \end{bmatrix}\begin{bmatrix} x \\ 3 \end{bmatrix} = O$, then value of x is

(a) $0, -\dfrac{3}{2}$ (b) $-\dfrac{3}{2}$

(c) $0, \dfrac{3}{2}$ (d) $0, -\dfrac{2}{3}$

15. If $P(x) = \begin{bmatrix} \cos x & \sin x \\ -\sin x & \cos x \end{bmatrix}$, then which of the following is true ?

(a) $P(x).\, P(y) = P(x - y)$ (b) $P(x).\, P(y) = P(x + y)$

(c) $P(x).\, P(y) = P(2x - y)$ (d) $P(x).\, P(y) = P(x - 2y)$

16. If $A = \begin{bmatrix} 0 & 0 \\ 2 & 0 \end{bmatrix}$, then $A^6 =$

(a) $\begin{bmatrix} 0 & 0 \\ 64 & 0 \end{bmatrix}$ (b) $\begin{bmatrix} 0 & 0 \\ 32 & 0 \end{bmatrix}$

(c) $\begin{bmatrix} 0 & 0 \\ 12 & 0 \end{bmatrix}$ (d) $\begin{bmatrix} 0 & 0 \\ 0 & 0 \end{bmatrix}$

17. If $A = \begin{bmatrix} 3 & -3 \\ -3 & 3 \end{bmatrix}$ and $A^2 = kA$, then value of k is

(a) 3   (b) 6

(c) 9   (d) 81

18. If $\begin{bmatrix} a+b & 2 \\ 5 & b \end{bmatrix} = \begin{bmatrix} 6 & 5 \\ 2 & 2 \end{bmatrix}^{T}$, then a = ?

(a) 2   (b) 6

(c) 4   (d) – 4

19. If $\begin{bmatrix} 0 & 2b & -2 \\ 3 & 1 & 3 \\ 3a & 3 & -1 \end{bmatrix}$ is a symmetric matrix , then the values of a and b are

(a) $-\dfrac{2}{3}, \dfrac{3}{2}$

(b) $\dfrac{2}{3}, \dfrac{3}{2}$

(c) $\dfrac{2}{3}, -\dfrac{3}{2}$

(d) $-\dfrac{2}{3}, -\dfrac{3}{2}$

20. If $\begin{bmatrix} 0 & a & -3 \\ 2 & 0 & -1 \\ b & 1 & 0 \end{bmatrix}$ is a skew-symmetric matrix , then the values of a and b are

(a) $-2, -3$

(b) $-2, 3$

(c) $2, -3$

(d) $-3, 3$

ANSWERS

Q. No.	1	2	3	4	5	6	7	8	9	10
Answer	(c)	(d)	(a)	(b)	(a)	(d)	(c)	(b)	(c)	(a)
Q. No.	11	12	13	14	15	16	17	18	19	20
Answer	(d)	(b)	(c)	(a)	(b)	(d)	(b)	(c)	(a)	(b)

DETERMINANTS

1. Let A be a square matrix of order 3×3 then $|KA|$ is equal to

(a) $K|A|$

(b) $K^2|A|$

(c) $K^3|A|$

(d) $2K|A|$

2. If $x \in N$ and $\begin{vmatrix} x+3 & -2 \\ -3x & 2x \end{vmatrix} = 8$, then find the value of x

(a) 3

(b) 2

(c) 7

(d) 1

3. If $\begin{vmatrix} 2 & 4 \\ 5 & 1 \end{vmatrix} = \begin{vmatrix} 2x & 4 \\ 6 & x \end{vmatrix}$, then value of x is

(a) 0

(b) $\pm\sqrt{2}$

(c) 1

(d) $\pm\sqrt{3}$

4. If $A = \begin{vmatrix} x & 2 \\ 2 & x \end{vmatrix}$ and $|A|^3 = 125$, then x is equal to

(a) ± 3

(b) ± 4

(c) ± 2

(d) ± 1

5. If A is a skew-symmetric matrix of order 3, then the value of $|A|$ is

(a) 3

(b) 0

(c) 9

(d) 27

6. If $\begin{vmatrix} 2 & 3 & 2 \\ x & x & x \\ 4 & 9 & 1 \end{vmatrix} + 3 = 0$, then the value of x is

(a) 3

(b) 0

(c) -1

(d) 1

94

7. If A is a square matrix such that $|A| = 5$, then the value of $|AA^T|$ is

(a) –5   (b) 125

(c) – 25   (d) 25

8. If area of triangle is 35 sq units with vertices $(2, -6)$, $(5, 4)$ and $(k, 4)$. Then k is

(a) –12, –2   (b) 12, –2

(c) –2   (d) 12

9. If A_{ij} is the co-factor of the element a_{ij} of the determinant $\begin{vmatrix} 2 & -3 & 5 \\ 6 & 0 & 4 \\ 1 & 5 & -7 \end{vmatrix}$, the value of $a_{32}.\,A_{32}$ is

(a) 11   (b) 32

(c) 110   (d) 113

10. If for any 2×2 square matrix A, $A(\text{adj } A) = \begin{bmatrix} 8 & 0 \\ 0 & 8 \end{bmatrix}$, then the value of $|A|$ is

(a) 64   (b) 8

(c) $2\sqrt{2}$ (d) 1

11. If A is a square matrix of order 3 such that $|\text{adj}A| = 64$, then value of $|A|$ is

(a) 4   (b) 8

(c) ± 4 (d) ± 8

12. If A is a square matrix of order 3, with $|A| = 9$, then the value of $|2.\text{adj } A|$ is

(a) 81   (b) 162

(c) 648   (d) 64

13. If $A = \begin{vmatrix} 2 & k & -3 \\ 0 & 2 & 5 \\ 1 & 1 & 3 \end{vmatrix}$, then A^{-1} exists if

(a) $k = 2$ (b) $k \neq 2$

(c) $k \neq \dfrac{8}{5}$ (d) $k \neq -\dfrac{8}{5}$

14. If A and B are matrices of order 3 and $|A| = 4$, $|B| = 5$, then $|3AB| =$

(a) 60   (b) 15

(c) 12   (d) 120

15. If A and B are invertible matrices, then which of the following is not correct?

(a) $\text{adj } A = |A|.\,A^{-1}$ (b) $\det(A)^{-1} = [\det(A)]^{-1}$

(c) $(A + B)^{-1} = B^{-1} + A^{-1}$ (d) $(AB)^{-1} = B^{-1} A^{-1}$

ANSWERS

Q. No.	1	2	3	4	5	6	7	8	9	10
Answer	(c)	(b)	(d)	(a)	(b)	(c)	(d)	(b)	(c)	(b)
Q. No.	11	12	13	14	15					
Answer	(d)	(c)	(d)	(a)	(c)					

CONTINUITY& DIFFERENTIABILITY
Multiple Choice Questions [MCQ]

1. Function $f(x) = \begin{cases} 2x-3, & \text{if } x < 2 \\ 5x-9, & \text{if } x \geq 2 \end{cases}$ is a continuous function:

(a) for all real value of x such that x ≠2.

(b) for all integral value of x only.

(c) for all real value of x.

(d) for x = 2 only.

2. Which of the following is not continuous for all $x \in R$:

(a) the constant function f (x) = k

(b) The identity function, i.e. f (x) = x

(c) the modulus function f given by f(x) = | x |

(d) the greatest integer function f (x) = [x]

3. Which of the following is not continuous for all $x \in R$

(a) f(x) = sinx

(b) f(x) = tanx

(c) A polynomial function

(d) A rational function $f(x) = \dfrac{p(x)}{q(x)}, q(x) \neq 0$

4. If f and g be two real functions continuous at a real number c. Then which of the following is not true

(a) f + g is continuous at x = c.

(b) f – g is continuous at x = c.

(c) f . g is not continuous at x = c.

(d) $\dfrac{f}{g}$ is continuous at x = c, (provided g (c)≠0).

5. All the points of discontinuity of the function f defined by f(x) = $\begin{cases} 3, & \text{if } 0 \leq x \leq 1 \\ 4, & \text{if } 1 < x < 3 \\ 5, & \text{if } 3 \leq x \leq 10 \end{cases}$

(a) 1, 3, 10

(b) 3, 10

(c) 0, 1, 3

(d) 1, 3

6. The function $f(x) = \dfrac{9-x^2}{9x-x^3}$ is

(a) discontinuous at only one point

(b) discontinuous at exactly two points

(c) discontinuous at exactly three points

(d) none of these

7. If $f(x) = \begin{cases} x^{10}-1, & \text{if } x \leq 1 \\ x^2, & \text{if } x > 1 \end{cases}$, then which of the following is not true

(a) continuous at all points x, such that x < 1

(b) continuous at all points x, such that x > 1

(c) continuous at x = 1

(d) continuous at x = 2

8. The value of k for which $f(x) = \begin{cases} \dfrac{1-\cos 4x}{2x^2}, & x \neq 0 \\ k, & x = 0 \end{cases}$ is continuous at x = 0 is :

(a) k = 1

(b) k = 2

(c) k = 0

(d) k = 4

9. The value of k for which $f(x) = \begin{cases} \dfrac{\sqrt{1+kx} - \sqrt{1-kx}}{x}, & -1 \leq x < 0 \\ \dfrac{2x+1}{x-1}, & 0 \leq x \leq 1 \end{cases}$ is continuous at x = 0 is :

(a) k = 0

(b) $k = \dfrac{1}{2}$

(c) $k = -\dfrac{1}{2}$

(d) k = 2

96

10. The value of k for which $f(x) = \begin{cases} \dfrac{\sqrt{1+kx} - \sqrt{1-kx}}{x}, & -1 \le x < 0 \\ \dfrac{2x+1}{x-1}, & 0 \le x \le 1 \end{cases}$ is continuous at x = 0 is :

(a) k = 0

(b) $k = \dfrac{1}{2}$

(c) k = −1

(d) k = 1

11. The value of k for which $f(x) = \begin{cases} \dfrac{kx}{|x|}, & \text{if } x < 0 \\ 3, & \text{if } x \ge 0 \end{cases}$ is continuous at x = 0 is :

(a) k = −3

(b) $k = \dfrac{1}{2}$

(c) k = −1

(d) k = 1

12. The value of k for which $f(x) = \begin{cases} \dfrac{(x+3)^2 - 36}{x-3}, & \text{if } x \ne 0 \\ k, & \text{if } x = 0 \end{cases}$ is continuous at x = 3 is :

(a) k = 2

(b) k = 12

(c) k = −1

(d) k = 6

13. The value of k for which $f(x) = \begin{cases} kx + 1, & \text{if } x \le \pi \\ \cos x, & \text{if } x > \pi \end{cases}$ is continuous at x = π is :

(a) $k = -\dfrac{2}{\pi}$

(b) $k = \dfrac{2}{\pi}$

(c) k = π

(d) $k = \dfrac{\pi}{2}$

14. The value of k for which $f(x) = \begin{cases} k(x^2 - 2x), & \text{if } x \le 0 \\ 4x + 1, & \text{if } x > 0 \end{cases}$ is continuous at x = 0 is :

(a) 1

(b) − 1

(c) 0

(d) none of these

15. The value of k for which $f(x) = \begin{cases} \dfrac{\sin 5x}{x^2 + 2x}, & \text{if } x \ne 0 \\ k + 1, & \text{if } x = 0 \end{cases}$ is continuous at x = 0 is :

(a) 1

(b) − 2

(c) $k = \dfrac{3}{2}$

(d) $\dfrac{1}{2}$

16. The greatest integer function defined by f(x) = [x], 0 < x < 3
(a) not differentiable at x = 1 only
(b)) not differentiable at x = 2 only
(c) not differentiable at x = 1, x = 2
(d) differentiable at x = 1, x = 2

17. The function f(x) = |x − 2| is
(a) neither continuous nor derivable at 2
(b) continuous but not derivable at 2
(c) continuous and derivable at 2
(d) none of these

18. If a function f(x) is defined as $f(x) = \begin{cases} \dfrac{x}{\sqrt{x^2}}, & \text{if } x \ne 0 \\ 0, & \text{if } x = 0 \end{cases}$ then :

(a) f(x) is discontinuous at x = 0

(b) f(x) is continuous as well as differentiable at x = 0

(c) f(x) is continuous at x = 0 but not differentiable at x = 0

(d) none of these

19. $\dfrac{d}{dx}\left[\sin^2\left(\sqrt{\cos x}\right)\right]=$

(a) $-\dfrac{2\sin x.\sin(\sqrt{\cos x}).\cos(\sqrt{\cos x})}{2(\sqrt{\cos x})}$

(b) $-\dfrac{2.\sin(\sqrt{\cos x}).\cos(\sqrt{\cos x})}{2(\sqrt{\cos x})}$

(c) $-\dfrac{2\sin x.\sin(\sqrt{\cos x})}{2(\sqrt{\cos x})}$

(d) $-\dfrac{2\sin x.\sin(\sqrt{\cos x}).\cos(\sqrt{\cos x})}{2}$

20. $\dfrac{d}{dx}\left[\log\sin\sqrt{x^2+1}\right]=$

(a) $\dfrac{2x\cos\sqrt{x^2+1}}{\sqrt{x^2+1}.\sin\sqrt{x^2+1}}$

(b) $\dfrac{x\cos\sqrt{x^2+1}}{2\sqrt{x^2+1}.\sin\sqrt{x^2+1}}$

(c) $\dfrac{\cos\sqrt{x^2+1}}{2\sqrt{x^2+1}.\sin\sqrt{x^2+1}}$

(d) $\dfrac{x\cos\sqrt{x^2+1}}{\sqrt{x^2+1}.\sin\sqrt{x^2+1}}$

21. $\dfrac{d}{dx}\left[2^{-x}\right]=$

(a) $\dfrac{1}{2^x}\log 2$

(b) $-\dfrac{1}{2^x}\log 2$

(c) $2^x\log 2$

(d) $-\dfrac{x}{2^{x+1}}$

22. $\dfrac{d}{dx}\left[e^{1+\log_e x}\right]=$

(a) 1

(b) 0

(c) $x.\log_e x$

(d) e

23. $\dfrac{d}{dx}\left[2^{\cos^2 x}\right]=$

(a) $2^{\cos^2 x}.\sin 2x$

(b) $-2^{\cos^2 x}.\log 2.\sin 2x$

(c) $2^{\cos^2 x}.\log 2.\sin 2x$

(d) $-2^{\cos^2 x}.\sin^2 x$

24. $\dfrac{d}{dx}\left[\log_e\tan\left(\dfrac{\pi}{4}+\dfrac{x}{2}\right)\right]=$

(a) sec x

(b) tanx

(c) secx.tanx

(d) $\sec^2 x$

25. $\dfrac{d}{dx}\left[\tan^{-1}\left(\dfrac{\sqrt{1+x^2}-1}{x}\right)\right]=$

(a) $\dfrac{\sqrt{1+x^2}}{x}$

(b) $\dfrac{1}{\left(1+x^2\right)}$

(c) $\dfrac{x}{\sqrt{1+x^2}-1}$

(d) $\dfrac{1}{2\left(1+x^2\right)}$

26. $\dfrac{d}{dx}\left[\sin^{-1}\left(\dfrac{1}{\sqrt{1+x^2}}\right)\right]=$

(a) $\dfrac{1}{1+x^2}$

(b) $-\dfrac{x}{1+x^2}$

(c) $-\dfrac{1}{1+x^2}$

(d) $-\dfrac{2x}{1+x^2}$

27. $\dfrac{d}{dx}\left[\tan^{-1}\left(\sqrt{\dfrac{1+\sin x}{1-\sin x}}\right)\right]=$ where $0 < x < \dfrac{\pi}{4}$

(a) $-\dfrac{1}{2}$

(b) $\dfrac{1}{2}$

(c) $\dfrac{1+\sin x}{1-\sin x}$

(d) $\dfrac{1-\sin x}{1+\sin x}$

28. $\dfrac{d}{dx}\left[\sin^{-1}\left(\dfrac{\sin x+\cos x}{\sqrt{2}}\right)\right]=$

(a) $\dfrac{1}{\sqrt{2}}$

(b) $\sqrt{2}$

(c) 1

(d) $-\sqrt{2}$

29. $\dfrac{d}{dx}\left[x^{\sin x}\right]=$

(a) $x^{\sin x}\left(\cos x+\dfrac{\sin x}{x}\right)$

(b) $x^{\sin x-1}.\cos x$

(c) $x^{\sin x}\left(\cos x.\log_e x+\sin x\right)$

(d) $x^{\sin x}\left(\cos x.\log_e x+\dfrac{\sin x}{x}\right)$

30. If $(\cos x)^y=(\sin y)^x$, then $\dfrac{dy}{dx}=$

(a) $\dfrac{\log\sin y+y\tan x}{(\log\cos x-x\cot y)}$

(b) $\dfrac{\log\sin y+\tan x}{(\log\cos x-x\cot y)}$

(c) $\dfrac{\log\sin y+y\tan x}{(\log\cos x+x\cot y)}$

(d) $\dfrac{\log\sin y+y\tan x}{(\log\cos x-\cot y)}$

31. If $y^x=e^{y-x}$, then $\dfrac{dy}{dx}=$.

(a) $\dfrac{y^x}{\log y}$

(b) $\dfrac{\log y}{(1+\log y)^2}$

(c) $\dfrac{(1+\log y)^2}{\log y}$

(d) $\dfrac{1}{\log y.(1+\log y)^2}$

32. $\dfrac{d}{dx}\left[x^{x^x}\right]=$

(a) $x^{x^x}.x^{x-1}$

(b) $x^{x^{x-1}}$

(c) $x^{x^x}.x^x\left[(1+\log x)\log x\right]$

(d) $x^{x^x}.x^x\left[(1+\log x)\log x+\dfrac{1}{x}\right]$

33. If $x = a(\theta - \sin\theta),\ y = a(1+\cos\theta)$, then $\dfrac{d^2y}{dx^2}$ at $\theta = \dfrac{\pi}{2}$ is equal to

(a) a

(b) $\dfrac{1}{a}$

(c) $\dfrac{1}{2a}$

(d) $\dfrac{2}{a}$

34. If $y = \sqrt{x+\sqrt{x+\sqrt{x+........\infty}}}$, then $\dfrac{dy}{dx} =$

(a) $\dfrac{1}{2y-1}$

(b) $\dfrac{1}{2y+1}$

(c) $\dfrac{1}{1-2y}$

(d) $\dfrac{2}{2y-1}$

35. If $y = \sqrt{\cos x + \sqrt{\cos x + \sqrt{\cos x + ...\infty}}}$, then $\dfrac{dy}{dx} =$

(a) $\dfrac{\cos x}{1-2y}$

(b) $\dfrac{\sin x}{1+2y}$

(c) $\dfrac{\sin x}{1-2y}$

(d) $\dfrac{\cos x}{1-2y}$

36. If $y = \left(x+\sqrt{x^2+a^2}\right)^n$, then $\dfrac{dy}{dx} =$

(a) $\dfrac{y}{n\sqrt{x^2+a^2}}$

(b) $\dfrac{ny}{\sqrt{x^2+a^2}}$

(c) $2nx\left(x+\sqrt{x^2+a^2}\right)^{n-1}$

(d) $\dfrac{y}{\sqrt{x^2+a^2}}$

37. If $x = a(\cos t + t\sin t)$ and $y = a(\sin t - t\cos t),\ 0 < t < \dfrac{\pi}{2}$, then $\dfrac{d^2x}{dt^2} =$

(a) $a(\cos t - t\sin t)$

(b) $at\sin t$

(c) $t\sin t$

(d) $a(\cos t + t\sin t)$

38. If $y = a\cos(\log x) + b\sin(\log x)$, then

(a) $x^2\dfrac{d^2y}{dx^2} + x\dfrac{dy}{dx} - y = 0$

(b) $x^2\dfrac{d^2y}{dx^2} - x\dfrac{dy}{dx} + y = 0$

(c) $x^2\dfrac{d^2y}{dx^2} + x\dfrac{dy}{dx} + y = 0$

(d) $x^2\dfrac{d^2y}{dx^2} - x\dfrac{dy}{dx} - y = 0$

39. If $x^m.y^n = (x+y)^{m+n}$, then $\dfrac{dy}{dx} =$

(a) $-\dfrac{y}{x}$

(b) $\dfrac{2y}{x}$

(c) $\dfrac{x}{y}$

(d) $\dfrac{y}{x}$

40. If $y = A\cos nx + B\sin nx$, then

(a) $\dfrac{d^2y}{dx^2} - n^2y = 0$

(b) $\dfrac{d^2y}{dx^2} + n^2y = 0$

(c) $\dfrac{d^2y}{dx^2} + y = 0$

(d) $\dfrac{d^2y}{dx^2} = n^2y^2$

ANSWERS

Q. No.	1	2	3	4	5	6	7	8	9	10
Answer	(c)	(d)	(b)	(c)	(d)	(b)	(c)	(d)	(c)	(c)
Q. No.	11	12	13	14	15	16	17	18	19	20
Answer	(a)	(b)	(a)	(d)	(c)	(c)	(b)	(a)	(a)	(d)
Q. No.	21	22	23	24	25	26	27	28	29	30
Answer	(b)	(d)	(b)	(a)	(d)	(c)	(b)	(c)	(d)	(a)
Q. No.	31	32	33	34	35	36	37	38	39	40
Answer	(c)	(d)	(b)	(a)	(c)	(b)	(a)	(c)	(d)	(b)

APPLICATION OF DERIVATIVE
INCREASING AND DECREASING FUNCTIONS
Multiple Choice Questions [MCQ]

1. If I be an open interval contained in the domain of a real valued function f and if $x_1 < x_2$ in I, then which of the following statements is true?

(a) f is said to be increasing on I, if $f(x_1) \le f(x_2)$ for all $x_1, x_2 \in I$

(b) f is said to be strictly increasing on I, if $f(x_1) < f(x_2)$ for all $x_1, x_2 \in I$

(c) Both (a) and (b) are true   (d) Both (a) and (b) are false

2. The function given by $f(x) = \cos x$ is

(a) strictly decreasing in $(0, \pi)$ (b) strictly increasing in $(\pi, 2\pi)$,

(c) neither increasing nor decreasing in $(0, 2\pi)$.   (d) none of the above

3. The function $f(x) = 4x + 3$, $x \in R$ is an

(a) increasing function   (b) decreasing function

(c) neither increasing nor decreasing   (d) none of the above

4. Function f given by $f(x) = x^2 - x + 1$ is

(a) strictly decreasing in $(-1, 1)$.   (b) strictly increasing in $(-1, 1)$.

(c) neither increasing nor decreasing in $(-1, 1)$.   (d) none of the above

5. The least value of a such that the function f given by $f(x) = x^2 + ax + 1$ is strictly increasing on $(1, 2)$ is

(a) $a = -3$ (b) $a = -2$

(c) $a = -2$ (d) $a = 3$

6. The function given by $f(x) = x^3 - 3x^2 + 3x - 100$ is

(a) increasing in **R**.   (b) decreasing in **R**

(c) neither increasing nor decreasing in **R**   (d) none of the above

7. The function $f(x) = \tan x - 4x$ is

(a) strictly increasing on $\left(-\dfrac{\pi}{3}, \dfrac{\pi}{3}\right)$ (b) strictly decreasing on $\left(-\dfrac{\pi}{3}, \dfrac{\pi}{3}\right)$

(c) neither increasing nor decreasing on $\left(-\dfrac{\pi}{3}, \dfrac{\pi}{3}\right)$ (d) none of the above

8. The interval in which $y = x^2 e^{-x}$ is increasing is

(a) $(-\infty, \infty)$ (b) $(-2, 0)$

(c) $(2, \infty)$ (d) $(0, 2)$

9. The function $f(x) = \log(\cos x)$ is

(a) strictly increasing on $\left(0, \dfrac{\pi}{2}\right)$ (b) strictly decreasing on $\left(0, \dfrac{\pi}{2}\right)$

(c) neither increasing nor decreasing on $\left(0, \dfrac{\pi}{2}\right)$ (d) none of the above

10. The interval for which the function $f(x) = \cot^{-1} x + x$ increases is

(a) $\left(0, \dfrac{\pi}{2}\right)$ (b) $\left(-\dfrac{\pi}{2}, \dfrac{\pi}{2}\right)$

(c) $(0, \pi)$ (d) $(-\infty, \infty)$

11. For which values of x, the function $y = x^4 - \dfrac{4x^3}{3}$ is increasing and for which values, it is decreasing.

(a) increasing in$(-\infty, 1]$ and decreasing in $[1, \infty)$ (b) increasing in $[1, \infty)$ and decreasing in $(-\infty, 1]$
(c) increasing in $[2, \infty)$ and decreasing in $(-\infty, 2]$ (d) (d) None of these

12. The interval on which the function $f(x) = 2x^3 + 9x^2 + 12x - 1$ is decreasing is
(a) $[-1, \infty]$ (b) $[-2, -1]$
(c) $[-\infty, -2]$ (d) $[-1, 1]$

13. The values of x for which the function $f(x) = 2 + 3x - x^3$ is decreasing is
(a) $x \le -2$ or $x \ge 2$ (b) $x \le 0$ or $x \ge 1$
(c) $x \le -1$ or $x \ge 1$ (d) none of these

14. The function $f(x) = 4x^3 - 18x^2 + 27x - 7$ is
(a) always decreasing in R. (b) neither increasing nor decreasing in R.
(c) always increasing in R. (d) none of these

15. The function f given by $f(x) = \tan^{-1}(\sin x + \cos x)$ is
(a) increasing for all $x \in (\pi/4, \pi/2)$ (b) decreasing for all $x \in (\pi/4, \pi/2)$
(c) neither increasing nor decreasing for $x \in (\pi/4, \pi/2)$ (d) none of these

ANSWERS

Q. No.	1	2	3	4	5	6	7	8	9	10
Answer	(c)	(d)	(a)	(c)	(b)	(a)	(b)	(d)	(b)	(d)
Q. No.	11	12	13	14	15					
Answer	(b)	(b)	(c)	(c)	(b)					

MAXIMA & MINIMA
Multiple Choice Questions [MCQ]

1. f be a function defined on an interval I. Then, which of the following is incorrect ?
(a) f is said to have a maximum value in I, if $\exists$ c in I such that $f(c) \ge f(x)$, $\forall x \in I$.
(b) f is said to have a minimum value in I, if $\exists$ c in I such that $f(c) \le f(x)$, $\forall x \in I$.
(c) f is said to have an extreme value in I, if $\exists$ t in I such that $f(c)$ is either a maximum or a minimum value of f in I.
(d) none of these

2. The maximum and minimum values of the function $f(x) = (2x - 1)^2 + 7$ are
(a) minimum Value = 5, no maximum (b) minimum Value = 7, no maximum
(c) no maximum Value = 3, maximum=1 (d) neither minimum nor maximum

3. The maximum and minimum values of the function $f(x) = 9x^2 + 12x + 2$ are
(a) minimum Value = 23, no maximum (b) minimum Value = -2, no maximum
(c) maximum Value = -2, no Minimum (d) neither minimum nor maximum

4. The maximum and minimum values of the function $f(x) = -(x-1)^2 + 10$ are
(a) minimum Value = 5, no maximum (b) maximum Value = 10, maximum=1
(c) maximum Value = 10, no minimum (d) neither minimum nor maximum

5. The maximum and minimum values of the function $f(x) = |\sin 4x + 3|$ are
(a) Minimum = 3 ; Maximum = 4 (b) Minimum = 0; Maximum = 4
(c) Minimum = 2; Maximum = 4 (d) none of these

6. The local maxima and local minima for $f(x) = x^3 - 3x$ are
(a) local minimum at x = 1 is -2, local maximum at x = -1, is 2
(b) local minimum at x = 1 is 2, local maximum at x = -1, is 3
(c) local minimum at x = 1 is -2, no local maximum
(d) none of these

103

7. The local maxima and local minima for $f(x) = x^3 - 6x^2 + 9x + 15$ are

(a) local minimum at $x = 3$ is 15, local maximum at $x = 1$, is 19

(b) local minimum at $x = 1$ is 2, local maximum at $x = 3$, is 3

(c) local minimum at $x = 1$ is -2 and no local maximum

(d) none of these

8. The absolute maximum value and the absolute minimum value of $f(x) = \sin x + \cos x$, $x \in [0, \pi]$

(a) Absolute minimum value = 1, absolute maximum value = $\sqrt{2}$

(b) Absolute minimum value = -1, absolute maximum value = $\sqrt{2}$

(c) Absolute minimum value = -1, absolute maximum value = 2

(d) none of these

9. The absolute maximum value and the absolute minimum value of $f(x) = (x-1)^2 + 3$, $x \in [-3, 1]$

(a) Absolute minimum value = 1, absolute maximum value = 19

(b) Absolute minimum value = 1, absolute maximum value = $\sqrt{2}$

(c) Absolute minimum value = -1, absolute maximum value = 19

(d) None of these

10. The minimum and maximum value of the function $\sin x + \cos x$ is

(a) Minimum = 0, maximum = $\sqrt{2}$ (b) Minimum = $-\sqrt{2}$, maximum = $\sqrt{2}$

(c) Minimum = $-\sqrt{2}$, maximum = 0   (d) None of these

ANSWERS

Q. No.	1	2	3	4	5	6	7	8	9	10
Answer	(d)	(b)	(b)	(c)	(c)	(a)	(a)	(b)	(a)	(b)

REFERENCES

1. https://ncert.nic.in/textbook.php
2. https://www.cbse.gov.in/cbsenew/question-paper.html

Printed in Great Britain
by Amazon

24245766R00059